Extravaganza One Act Fest 2024

A Collection of Original One-Act Plays

"You don't become an artist

by thinking about it.

You become one

by doing the work."

Foreword from the Director

The stories you are about to read didn't begin with a script. They began with a point of view. An impulse. A question. A need to say something that couldn't be ignored.

This festival was built on that foundation.

The 2024 Extravaganza One-Act Festival is not a collection of finished pieces that arrived polished and complete. It is the result of artists stepping into the unknown and doing the work—day after day, moment after moment—until something honest revealed itself. Every piece was created from the ground up. No shortcuts. No safety net. Just actors, writers, and directors committing to the process in a creative laboratory where ideas were tested, challenged, broken apart, and rebuilt, where actors were asked not just to perform, but to create, to take ownership, to bring their full point of view into the room and stand behind it.

That's what makes this a laboratory. And that's what connects it to the spirit of TesserAct Theater Company —a space where artists don't wait for opportunity, they generate it. Where ideas aren't protected, they're pressure-tested. Where the goal isn't to look like an artist…

…it's to be one.

Wolfgang Bodison

Table of Contents

Foreword from the Director................................IV

THE RAT RACE..6

DEMON CORE..22

CANCEL QUEEN..39

COLD BLOODED..62

BABY ELLA..77

BREAKING THE LINE..89

THE RAT RACE

by Sophie Steele and Natalia Montgomery

Overview
a 15-minute comedy
for 5 actors, 2 female, 1 male, 2 any gender

Synopsis
A naive secretary tries her best to keep her unhinged
predecessor from breaking a restraining order and
attacking her boss, until discoveries about his shady
business practices come to light.

Characters
CLAIRE PRESCOTT – female, mid 20s,
         Gerald's previous assistant
VIVIAN MALLOY – female, early 20s,
         Gerald's current assistant
GERALD FONTZ – male, 30s, marketing director
GUARD 1   – any gender, 20s to 50s
GUARD 2   – any gender, 20s to 50s

Setting
The reception of a marketing office, present day.

Notes
Set: desk with a chair, couch, two slipper chairs, small
coffee table, bookshelf
Props: sandwich, takeout coffee cup, wireless desk
phone, long power cord, shoulder bag with folders and

papers, two laptops, handcuffs, Bluetooth phone headset

The fight choreography described here was appropriate to the space in which this play was originally staged. Use your creativity and your resources to create a fight that suits your stage. It should, however, be an incredibly physical, comedically violent fight. Similarly, the stage setup described here can be altered to fit the needs of the space.

Music Use Note

Licensees must secure permission for any copyrighted music or use only original music they own. All music clearances are the licensee's responsibility, and they agree to indemnify the copyright owners and licensing agent against any related claims.

Original Premiere

The Rat Race premiered on June 8th, 2024, at the 2024 Extravaganza One Act Fest, directed by Wolfgang Bodison.

Original Cast

CLAIRE PRESCOTT   – Sophie Steele
VIVIAN MALLOY   – Natalia Montgomery
GERALD FONTZ   – Will Hart
GUARD 1   – Sonny Schnapf
GUARD 2   – Joe Purcell

Performance Rights

This play may not be performed, reproduced, or adapted without written permission from the author. To request performance rights, please send a request through https://nataliamontgomery.wordpress.com/contact-form/

Sophie Steele and Natalia Montgomery,
photo by Grant Terzakis

Scene 1

Lights up. A desk and office chair are downstage right. A bookshelf is upstage right. A couch is upstage center. Two slipper chairs and a coffee table are stage left. There is a plaque reading "Gerald Fontz Director of Marketing" next to a door upstage left. "The Girl from Ipanema" or similar soft elevator music plays. Vivian sits at the desk and alternates between typing and eating a sandwich. Claire, in sunglasses and a hat, sneaks onstage from the audience entrance, looking behind her and carrying a take-out coffee cup. Vivian watches her in confusion as she walks into the room.

VIVIAN. Excuse me, miss, can I help you?
CLAIRE. Oh my god! Wait, what are you doing here?
VIVIAN. I work here? I'm sorry, who are you?

Claire tries to hide behind the coffee.

CLAIRE. Oh, um… *(disguising her voice)* Just delivering a coffee for Mr. Fontz, excuse me…

Claire tries to walk by Vivian's desk and through the office door, but Vivian blocks her entry.

VIVIAN. I'm sorry, Mr. Fontz is currently in a meeting and I can't let anyone in there without his permission.

CLAIRE. Don't worry about it, I'm just going to put this on his desk and go. I'll just be a minute– more like a second.

Vivian tries to guide Claire to one of the chairs but Claire maneuvers around her. Vivian continues to get between her and the door.

VIVIAN. Well, I can't let anyone in who hasn't been approved by Mr. Fontz, but you can just wait here–

CLAIRE. (*normal voice*) Oh my god, Vivian, just let me through!

VIVIAN. How did you… Wait a minute. Claire?! You're not supposed to be here!

Claire sets the cup down on Vivian's desk and pulls off her hat, sunglasses, and shoulder bag.

CLAIRE. No, you're not supposed to be here! It's 1 PM, shouldn't you be on your lunch break?

VIVIAN. I had some work to catch up on. I was eating at my desk.

CLAIRE. He was always trying to get me to do that, too. You know that's illegal, right?

Claire starts walking quickly towards the door. Vivian wraps her arms around Claire, trying to pull her back. The struggle should develop with the dialogue until Vivian is pulling Claire by her leg while Claire hangs onto the couch for dear life.

VIVIAN. Claire, I'm sorry but you can't be here. The restraining order clearly states you can't be within twenty feet–

CLAIRE. That order is bullshit–

VIVIAN. Are you kidding?! You killed his cat!

CLAIRE. HE'S STILL TELLING PEOPLE THAT?

VIVIAN. And you set his lawn on fire.

CLAIRE. That was an accident!

VIVIAN. And you carved the word "ASSHOLE" into the side of his car.

CLAIRE. That one was good. And don't try to tell me he's not the biggest asshole you've ever met.

VIVIAN. Look, it doesn't matter whether or not I think he's an asshole. Don't make me call security.

The phone on Vivian's desk rings and she instinctively turns towards it.

CLAIRE. Well, aren't you Miss Perfect Little Assistant.

VIVIAN. You would know. You trained me.

CLAIRE. Well, if I had known I was gonna get fired within a month, I wouldn't have done such a damn good job! You better get that, Miss Priss, you know what happens if you miss a call.

The phone keeps ringing. Vivian starts moving to answer it.

VIVIAN. You're right. And I can tell the person on the phone to send security up here.

Time slows down. The women move in slow motion, racing for the phone. "The Girl From

Ipanema" plays distortedly. Vivian is winning until Claire shoves her face and Vivian falls to the floor. Claire sits at the desk and answers the phone as time and the music speed back up to normal.

CLAIRE. *(sweetly)* Gerald Fontz's office, please hold. *(She hangs up.)* Look, Viv, you just let me in there for two seconds, I give him the coffee, and I'm out. Gone forever. You won't see me again.

Vivian pulls the chair out from under Claire and starts shoving it under the doorknob to Gerald's office.

VIVIAN. You know I can't do that. And don't call me Viv.
CLAIRE. Viv. Come on. We're pals, aren't we? Do it for old times' sake.
VIVIAN. I can't get fired.
CLAIRE. You're not gonna get fired! Just say I overpowered you. "Oh, Mr. Fontz, she was too strong! I simply couldn't hold her back from the door!"

With the chair positioned, Vivian stands between Claire and the door. Claire, head down, runs full force at her. Vivian catches Claire's head and holds her at arm's length until she gives up.

VIVIAN. Yeah, that sounds like a great plan.

CLAIRE. I'll fake wrestle you for it. I'll make it look super realistic, don't worry. You can even punch me in the face once if you want.

Claire tries to put Vivian in a headlock. Vivian pushes Claire bodily away from her.

VIVIAN. Absolutely not.
CLAIRE. You're killing me, Viv!

Vivian sits in the chair and Claire slumps to the floor while they both catch their breath. Claire gets up and gets a drink from the bar, and offers one to Vivian which she turns down.

VIVIAN. What's with the coffee anyway? You must know he'd never sit down to talk to you, right?
CLAIRE. Well, he isn't supposed to know it's from me.
VIVIAN. What?

The phone rings again as both women freeze and then make a break for the phone. They fight over the receiver until Vivian answers and hangs up.

VIVIAN. Gerald Fontz's office, please hold.
CLAIRE. GOD. You clearly just love your job here, keeping a tight lid on Mr. Big Man's calendar.
VIVIAN. I do more than just keep track of his appointments, okay?

Vivian tries to move the couch in front of the door but it's too heavy.

CLAIRE. Yeah I know, you probably still do his weekly mani/pedis. Does he still have that perpetual ingrown?

VIVIAN. No, I mean yes he does, but I mean I'm training to be an account manager now.

CLAIRE. Sure you are.

VIVIAN. Well, technically, I haven't started yet, but Gerald said once I finish training the new hire, I can move full-time onto Dave's team.

CLAIRE. Viv.

VIVIAN. What?

CLAIRE. *(manically)* Look at me: he is never letting you move into accounts management.

VIVIAN. Ok, Claire, I think you need to sit down maybe.

Vivian pulls Claire down onto the couch. Claire grabs Vivian's face and holds it an inch away from her own. She then pulls a bunch of papers out of her bag.

CLAIRE. No! I have proof! I followed up with his previous assistants and they all got fired within a month of asking for a transfer. You have access to the employment records, right?

VIVIAN. Yeah.

CLAIRE. Look them up right now and if there's any record of their transfers in the system, I'll leave right now, peacefully.

VIVIAN. Fine.

Claire guides Vivian back to the desk. Vivian looks up the records on her laptop.

CLAIRE. See? None of those transfers are in the
          system. Not even mine.
VIVIAN. You asked for a transfer?
CLAIRE. Yep. Asked to move to the art department.
          And then trained my replacement *(gesturing to
          Vivian)* just like you're training yours. I don't
          see your transfer in here either.
VIVIAN. *(pause)* That son of a bitch! I'm gonna kill
          him!

*Vivian turns to run towards the office door but
Claire grabs her arm and holds her back.*

CLAIRE. Woah wait! Wait!
VIVIAN. You've been trying to push past me this
          whole time and now you want to wait? Let's go
          rip him a new one.
CLAIRE. NO! I don't want to have a nice little chat
          with that snake!
VIVIAN. There will be no "nice little chatting". There
          will be righteous anger and then going to HR to
          get him fired!
CLAIRE. No, I have a whole plan. With the coffee,
          remember?
VIVIAN. Screw your weird coffee plan! I'm going in
          there!

*Claire shoves Vivian into the chair and starts
tying her up with an electrical cord. Once done,
she lies back on the couch, exhausted but
satisfied.*

CLAIRE. Viv, listen to me! Let's just say, two pumps
          of vanilla and a sprinkle of cinnamon aren't the
          only custom toppings in this latte.
VIVIAN. What, like… oh my god, did you pee in
          there?
CLAIRE. Ew no! I'm not an animal! It's just rat
          poison.
VIVIAN. Oh. *(beat)* Wait, what?!
CLAIRE. Yeah. I figure if he's gonna go around acting
          like a rat I may as well do some exterminating.
VIVIAN. You're trying to *murder* him?! Now I'm
          actually calling security.

*Vivian, still tied to the chair, scoots and
waddles to the desk and picks up the receiver.
Claire notices a second too late and runs to
catch up with her.*

CLAIRE. Vivian, no! What are you doing? You just
          said you wanted to kill him too!
VIVIAN. Well, I mean, yeah, but I wasn't being
          literal! I know you getting fired and the
          restraining order is a lot, but *murder*?!

*Claire and Vivian struggle over the phone until
Vivian succeeds.*

VIVIAN. *(into the phone)* Security to Mr. Fontz's
          office!
CLAIRE. Vivian, no! It's not murder! It's justice.
VIVIAN. So you're a vigilante now?
CLAIRE. You know who else was a vigilante?
          Batman. And you can be my Robin!

VIVIAN. Well, Batman was a billionaire who never got caught! We're gonna get caught. Why am I saying we?

CLAIRE. Viv, just think about it: you take him the coffee but they'll arrest me, and no one will suspect a thing! I'll be the fall guy and you'll be the one waiting for me until I get out of prison.

VIVIAN. Who says I won't go to prison too? If I give him a poisoned coffee, I'm an accessory to murder! I don't have the disposition for prison!

Vivian unties the cord and gets up from the chair.

CLAIRE. No prison for you, Viv! Just say, I talked you into letting me go in there and make amends with Ger. How were you supposed to know about the coffee? *(imitating Vivian in a nerdy voice and wringing her hands)* "How could this have happened? Maybe he's allergic!"

VIVIAN. I don't sound like that. Fine, let's say I don't know anything about it. My transfer still won't be in the system.

CLAIRE. So you tell Ger's replacement that you were supposed to get a transfer! What does he know?

VIVIAN. There's no guarantee the new guy will even consider letting me leave! Clearly, Gerald was only doing it to appease me until he could fire me.

CLAIRE. *(beat)* You're right. You're right. But with this coffee, it would be way easier for a 'transfer for Vivian Malloy to accounts management' to end up on his laptop than it is right now. I remember when I was training you…. I was like, "This girl's gonna go far. Nobody's gonna stand in her way."

Claire puts her arm around Vivian's shoulders.

CLAIRE. Now I'm gonna choke you out and give him the coffee anyway. I just hope for your sake, you find that girl in there somewhere again.

Suddenly, security bursts in from the audience entrance.

GUARD 1. Claire Prescott, you're trespassing and you need to leave immediately.

Both women freeze, then Vivian starts making choking noises while she maneuvers Claire's arm to make it look like Claire is choking her. Claire looks at her, confused for a moment, then joins in the facade.

VIVIAN. Help, she's choking me!
CLAIRE. Oh my god. Vivian Malloy! You foiled my master plan– my daring escape.

Claire shoves Vivian at the guards. Guard 1 gets out of the way and makes for Claire while she backs away. Vivian "accidentally" fully runs into Guard 2 and keeps them occupied.

CLAIRE. You'll never take me alive!
GUARD 1. Stop resisting!
CLAIRE. Never!

*Claire runs around the desk in circles from
Guard 1 while Guard 2 calms Vivian down.*

GUARD 2. I'm so sorry, Ms. Malloy, we've called the
　　　police. They'll be here any moment. Also, you
　　　should take the back exit when you leave
　　　tonight, the reporters are everywhere.
VIVIAN. Reporters?
GUARD 2. Someone set fire to the front lawn. It
　　　burned "Gerald Fontz is a twat". News teams
　　　got wind of it and sent out a bunch of camera
　　　crews.
VIVIAN. *(deadpan)* God, she's completely unhinged. I
　　　was terrified for my life.

*Guard 2 finally steps in and intercepts Claire
as she runs around the desk. She is subdued
with handcuffs. The guards start to hustle
Claire towards the audience entrance while she
fights them as best she can.*

GUARD 2. Well, I'm sure the whole firm is grateful
　　　for your considerable help catching this
　　　criminal–
CLAIRE. That's criminal mastermind to you– CURSE
　　　YOU, VIVIAN! I'll never forget you!

*Claire lets herself get dragged out by the
guards. Vivian raises a hand in farewell. A
greasy-haired man pokes his head out of the
office and pulls a Bluetooth phone headset out
of his ear.*

GERALD. What's all the commotion out here, Vivian? I don't pay you to throw parties in my waiting room.

VIVIAN. Oh, well, it's kind of a long story, but first I have a question–

GERALD. Oh, good, you got my afternoon coffee on time for once. You're not completely worthless. Such a good little secretary.

Gerald pats her on the head and grabs the coffee. Vivian moves to stop him, but then stops herself.

VIVIAN. I was wondering if we could discuss my transfer today?

GERALD. Oh, we can talk about that once you finish training Marta. Best not to overload you with a bunch of information just yet.

Gerald walks back to his office, taking a sip of the coffee, and shuts the door. Suddenly, choking sounds are heard. Vivian calmly dials the phone. While on the phone, she goes into Gerald's office and comes back out with a laptop.

VIVIAN. *(fake panic)* Hi, my boss is choking and he can't breathe! (...) I'm not sure. (...) Well, it started happening right after he drank some coffee. (...) No, I don't know what he's allergic to. (...) Yes, okay, we're on the fifth floor. (...) Please hurry!

She hangs up and starts dictating her typing.

VIVIAN. Transfer… Vivian… Malloy… to… accounts… management… department… effective… immediately.

She hits the enter key with gusto and smiles.

End of Play.

DEMON CORE

by Niki J. Borger

Overview
a 15-minute drama
for 3 actors, 2 female, 1 male, and 1 female voice-over

Synopsis
When a fatal accident leads to their father's radiation poisoning, two alienated sisters have to make amends to help him.

Characters

QUINN	– female, 20s to 30s
ARI	– female, 20s to 30s, Quinn's younger sister
DR BENNETT	– male, 30s to 50s
NURSE	– female, voice-over

Setting
The waiting area of the hospital at the military nuclear research facility in Los Alamos, New Mexico. May 22nd, 1946, one day after the accidental fission reaction of the Demon Core, a sphere of plutonium used to explore criticality.

Notes
Attire, demeanor, and accent should reflect the historical context of 1940s (not 50s!) post-war America. I suggest a transatlantic accent for both Ari and Quinn.

Original Premiere

Demon Core premiered on June 15th, 2024, at the 2024 Extravaganza One Act Fest, directed by Wolfgang Bodison.

Original Cast

QUINN   – Megan Corse
ARI   – Niki J. Borger
DR BENNETT   – Will Hart
NURSE   – Erin Hadfield

Performance Rights

This play may not be performed, reproduced, or adapted without written permission from the author. To request performance rights, please go to https://nikijborger.com/plays

Megan Corse and Niki J. Borger,
photo by Alisa Schulz

Scene 1

Lights up on a hospital waiting room. Center stage, a row of chairs with a small table in between. On one side of the stage, a little kitchenette with a water jug, coffee, glasses, cups, sugar, cream, and spoons.
ARI listens to the radio ("Shhh, it's a military secret") while she waits. After a moment, QUINN enters in a rush, while rearranging a folder under her jacket, so nobody can see it. She keeps searching her handbag and pockets.

ARI. *(screaming with excitement)* Quinn!
QUINN. Ari.
ARI. It is so good to see you! It has been way too long. You look splendid, if I may say so!

Ari rushes to hug Quinn, who drops the folder in the commotion. She quickly picks it up and hides it again, then continues searching her handbag.

QUINN. What are you doing here?
ARI. They flew me in this morning. What a rush! Have you ever traveled by air? Two soldiers came to the store, both of them so good-looking, and they said: Ma'am, we need you to come with us. And I said: Sir, if you want to take me, I shall not resist.
QUINN. What are you doing here?
ARI. They said it was urgent, but they didn't say why. What is going on? Is mother alright?
QUINN. In a moment. Would you happen to have a

clean handkerchief?

ARI. I am quite sure I do. What would you need it for?

QUINN. I will explain later. Please.

NURSE. (*over speaker*) Dr Bennett to Demon Core unit.

Ari starts searching her bag for a handkerchief when DR BENNETT enters on his way to the Demon Core unit.

BENNETT. Miss Sullivan, you're back. And you must be–

ARI. Ari Sullivan.

QUINN. My sister.

BENNETT. Nice to meet you. Dr Bennett.

ARI. Doctor, please explain why we are here. What is happening?

BENNETT. There has been an accident–

ARI. An accident, here? When?

BENNETT. Yesterday morning. It involved your father, Dr Sullivan.

ARI. What happened?

BENNETT. I have no authority to disclose that information.

ARI. Is he alright?

BENNETT. Your father has been exposed to a critical amount of radiation. He is currently suffering from acute radiation syndrome, and we are not quite sure yet–

ARI. Acute radiation syndrome, what does that mean?

BENNETT. There are a number of symptoms, including nausea, diarrhea–

ARI. Are you sure it's not just a stomach flu?

QUINN. Is he conscious yet?

BENNETT. I am afraid not.
QUINN. But you're expecting him to regain
        consciousness?
BENNETT. We are hoping for the best.
ARI. Hoping? What do you mean, hoping?
BENNETT. Have you ever experienced a sunburn?
ARI. Of course. Only last year, I was out tanning on
        Coney Island, you know, a nice swimsuit,
        matching sunnies, a great view of the local
        lifeguard – when I just fell asleep and woke up
        red like a tomato. What a disaster!

*Bennett and Quinn throw each other a glance
of disbelief.*

BENNETT. Your father is suffering from a three–
        dimensional sunburn, so to speak. And we don't
        yet know what the long-term effects of that will
        be.
NURSE. (*over speaker*) Dr Bennett to Demon Core
        unit.

Bennett starts leaving, but Quinn stops him.

QUINN. When can I see him?
BENNETT. Soon. Adequate measures are being
        prepared as we speak.
ARI. What measures?
BENNETT. I will explain more soon.
NURSE. *(over speaker)* Dr Bennett, please proceed to
        Demon Core unit immediately.
QUINN. Doctor, I was told that we would only get to
        see him once. Why is that?
BENNETT. Standard procedure here in Los Alamos.

He leaves.

QUINN. Ari, the handkerchief, if you don't mind.

Still staring after Bennett, Ari slowly starts searching her bag.

ARI. He certainly catches the eye. If I were to faint, do you think he would catch me?
QUINN. Ari, the handkerchief!

Ari pulls a handkerchief from her bag and gives it to Quinn. Quinn sits and starts searching her bag for a bottle of pills.

ARI. Demon Core, what a name! It sounds like the villain in some heroic story, like a Greek ethos! The beautiful, innocent maid is about to be eaten by the monstrous Demon Core, when a handsome, sturdy knight comes to save her!
QUINN. It's the name they gave the plutonium core he was working on, I think.

Quinn pours some of the pills onto the handkerchief, then folds it over.

ARI. So he was working with plutonium when it happened?
QUINN. Of course, he was. What else would he be doing?
ARI. How would I know?

Quinn places the handkerchief on the nearby table, looks around, then tries to crush the pills between her hands. It's not going too well.

ARI. What are you doing?

Quinn stops the crushing and starts moving toward Ari, who backs away toward the kitchenette.

QUINN. Why are you here, Ari?
ARI. Excuse me?
QUINN. Why are you here?
ARI. They insisted I come.
QUINN. I think it would be better if you were to leave.
ARI. He's my father, too, you know.
QUINN. Hasn't seemed like it recently.
ARI. Look, I understand that you're a little upset, and I am sorry I didn't move here with you.
QUINN. That's not what I'm talking about.
ARI. What are you talking about then?
QUINN. You left us, from one day to the next, no explanation, and you haven't visited once. You knew mother was sick, and you haven't called in a year.
ARI. I used to call.
QUINN. And then what?
ARI. She stopped answering the telephone.
QUINN. Exactly.
ARI. How is she? Why isn't she here?
QUINN. Because last week, she used the toaster to dry her hands.
ARI. Did it work? I'm joking! Why didn't you call me?
QUINN. Please stop pretending you care. I don't have the patience for it.

ARI. I do care.

> *Quinn reaches past Ari, takes a spoon from the kitchenette, and proceeds to crush the pills with it, ignoring Ari.*

ARI. How's your husband doing? Oh, that's right, you don't have one. Might be the way you're treating people...

> *Quinn ignores her.*

ARI. What "adequate measures" do they have to prepare? Quinn?

> *Still, Quinn ignores her. Ari attempts to grab the folder, but Quinn prevents it.*

ARI. Well, if you won't talk to me, I'm sure the handsome doctor will–

> *Ari starts making her way towards the hallway, when–*

QUINN. Radiation suits.
ARI. What's that?
QUINN. It will protect us from being exposed to the radiation.
ARI. I don't get it.
QUINN. As per usual.
ARI. Your tone is quite unnecessary.
QUINN. Radiation doesn't just go away. It's not like a virus that your immune system must battle and win. Once it's there, it is nearly impossible to

get rid of.

ARI. But they're helping him, aren't they? They're treating him.

QUINN. They're trying.

ARI. You don't think they are?

QUINN. I don't think they can.

ARI. You are being so dramatic. This is the American government! I'm sure they would tell us if things were that serious.

QUINN. No, I don't think they would.

ARI. What are you talking about? Quinn? What is that?

Ari takes the folder. Quinn attempts to get it back several times, with no success. Finally, Ari opens it, screams, and drops it onto the floor. Pictures of destruction and death fly everywhere. Quinn rushes to pick them up before anyone finds them. Slowly, Ari picks up the folder and scans it more closely.

ARI. What is this?

QUINN. It's what really happened in Japan. After they dropped the bombs.

ARI. Let me see! Where did you get this?

QUINN. I took it from father's office this morning.

ARI. I can't believe this.

QUINN. That's what radiation syndrome looks like.

ARI. Why is nobody talking about it?

QUINN. Can you imagine if this were made public?

ARI. That's how they won the war.

QUINN. That's how they ended the war.

ARI. And you got this from father?

QUINN. From his office, yes.

*Quinn grabs for the folder in Ari's hands, but
Ari pulls it away just in time.*

ARI. This is what he was working on?
QUINN. I think so.
ARI. This is the science he preferred to spend time on,
       over us.
QUINN. You're being dramatic.
ARI. This is why he made us move.
QUINN. Well, you never moved, did you, Ari!

*In one big lunge, Quinn takes the folder from
Ari, returns to the chairs, and hides it again.
Then she continues crushing the pills.*

ARI. Quinn, what are you doing?
QUINN. We have to help him.
ARI. I thought you said he cannot be helped?
QUINN. He cannot be healed, but he can be helped.

*Realization dawns on Ari's face as Quinn
checks on the pills being turned into powder.*

ARI. You're not serious.
QUINN. I'm deadly serious.
ARI. This isn't funny.
QUINN. Quite the opposite.
ARI. You want to kill our father.
QUINN. I want to relieve his suffering.

*Ari takes the bottle of pills from Quinn's open
handbag. Quinn walks to the kitchenette, as Ari
follows.*

ARI. What is this? Barbiturate? Why would you carry
      barbiturates in your handbag?
QUINN. Never you mind.
ARI. Tell me, Quinn!

Quinn fills a glass with water.

QUINN. My doctor gave them to me. I'm having
      trouble sleeping.
ARI. Since when?
QUINN. Since I served. As a nurse in the war. Trust
      me, I've seen enough cases like this.

Quinn drinks it.

ARI. You mean people suffering from radiation
      syndrome? I didn't know you–
QUINN. No, I mean people who had no chance of
      survival.
ARI. You don't know that for sure!

Quinn slams the empty glass onto the table.

QUINN. You don't understand, do you? For the last
      twenty-four hours, father has probably been
      vomiting uncontrollably, but there is nothing
      left to vomit. So now he's just choking, because
      his glands are too burned to even make saliva.
      The skin of his entire body is burned and
      blistering. Just lying on a mattress will cause
      him insufferable pain. Even his blood is burned.
      But nothing can be done about it, because his
      bones are too burned to make any new cells, to
      repair the damage. And because radiation

doesn't just go away, it will slowly disintegrate every organ and every cell of his body, until he's nothing but human mash. And he will feel every bit of it while it's happening. He is feeling every bit of it, as it's happening. Would you really want that on anyone, Ari? You've seen what it looks like. Do you want this on our father?

ARI. You know, right now, you look just like mother.

Quinn refills the glass with some water, then takes it back to the crushed pills.

ARI. Please, hold on for a moment.
QUINN. Why? Doctor Bennett will be back soon. And we only get one chance.
ARI. Do you think father knew they were going to drop the bombs on innocent families and children?
QUINN. Like I said, the folder is from his office.

Quinn pours the crushed pills into the water.

ARI. If he had his hands in this, he surely doesn't deserve our help now.
QUINN. Nobody deserves to die this way.
ARI. Maybe this is God making him pay for his sins.
QUINN. If there is a God, he's left this world a long time ago.
ARI. Isn't it ironic that father will die in the exact way as the people he killed?
QUINN. He didn't kill anyone.

Quinn takes the spoon to dissolve the pills in

the water.

ARI. He helped build the bombs.
QUINN. He did the job he was paid to do.
ARI. And that makes him not responsible?
QUINN. He provided for us! He allowed both of us to
        go to college. He loved us!
ARI. Speak for yourself! You were always his favorite!
QUINN. He is paying for mother's nurse and
        treatment.
ARI. Rightfully so, since he worsened her condition!
QUINN. Those bombs ended a horrific war. They kept
        us safe.
ARI. He didn't do that for us; he did it for himself!
QUINN. Without father, none of us would be here right
        now.
ARI. Precisely! Without father, none of us would be
        here right now! We would be back in Boston,
        mother would recognize our faces, and we'd all
        be happy!

*Ari, overcome by emotion, turns away from her
sister. A moment of silence. The barbiturate
powder is fully dissolved in the water now.*

ARI. You weren't there in the days before I left. You
        were away serving when father informed us
        that we would have to move here. And mother
        was so worried. She didn't want to leave. And
        her doctor said she shouldn't leave, it would be
        detrimental to her condition, but father decided
        to anyway. I hated to see mother in that state.
        So, I tried to talk to him. But he wouldn't hear

it. I became angry. I said I was tired of him treating us like we weren't even there. And then he slapped me. And told me to know my place.
QUINN. Ari, I'm so sorry that happened to you.
ARI. Sissy, I'm so sorry I left.

Quinn puts an arm around Ari.

QUINN. Just so you know, you were always my favorite sister.
ARI. I'm your only sister.
QUINN. And my favorite.

Dr Bennett returns from the Demon Core unit. Quinn immediately hides the glass with the dissolved pills and the syringe.

BENNETT. I have good news. We will have the radiation suits ready for you in just a few minutes. Unfortunately, you need to go in individually. The suits will protect you against radiation for a short period. However, you will not be allowed to approach your father closer than three feet, for your own safety.
ARI. Why can't we see him together?
BENNETT. Standard procedure here in Los Alamos. Miss Sullivan, given your previous status as a military nurse, we have approved your clearance to see him first. Any questions?

Quinn shakes her head. He leaves. Quinn moves towards the barbiturate solution, but Ari gets there first and takes it.

QUINN. Ari, it is now or never.
ARI. Quinn, I can't let you do this.
QUINN. We have to help him.
ARI. I have to talk to him first. I need a chance to
      make things right.
QUINN. It's too late, Ari. He won't even hear you, let
      alone answer.
ARI. It doesn't matter. I can't let that argument be our
      last memory together.
QUINN. Ari, he's dying. If you want to make things
      right, let me help him now.

      *Quinn takes the barbiturate mix from her, then
      she pulls a box with a syringe from her
      handbag.*

ARI. How would you even do it? We can't get closer
      than three feet.
QUINN. It has to be injected into a vein.

      Quinn takes out the syringe.

ARI. But that will be too close!
QUINN. I'll be wearing a suit. I'll take the risk.
ARI. You'll risk your own life to kill your father
      quicker than he would die anyway.
QUINN. I'll risk my own life to relieve his suffering.

      Quinn pulls the solution into the syringe.

ARI. This is insane.
QUINN. It's the right thing to do.
ARI. Father would not want you to risk your life for
      him. You just said he saved our lives. You can't

just throw that away.

*Quinn attaches the needle to the syringe, then
presses it until some of the liquid spills out at
the top.*

QUINN. I'm not throwing it away. I'm taking a
       calculated risk.
ARI. What about mother?
QUINN. She still has you, doesn't she? Doesn't she?

*They see Dr Bennett approaching. Quinn wraps
the handkerchief around the syringe, then slips
it into her handbag.*

ARI. Well then, what about me, Quinn?
QUINN. What about you?
ARI. You can't… You can't leave me alone with this
     mess. You can't all leave me.

Quinn cleans up all the evidence.

QUINN. Not too long ago, you were the one who left
       us.
ARI. And I've regretted it every day since.
QUINN. I know that Ari, but–
ARI. What if you get arrested? You're my favorite
     sister–
QUINN. I'm your only sister.

*Ari stops her and keeps her from moving by
holding onto her.*

ARI. Precisely! Promise me, you won't do it.

QUINN. Ari–
ARI. Please, Quinn!
QUINN. Ari, I–
ARI. Don't leave me!
BENNETT. (*to Quinn*) They're ready for you.
ARI. QUINN!
BENNETT. Miss Sullivan!
QUINN. Don't worry, I'll do the right thing. For all of
    us.

> *Quinn gently frees herself and leaves, handbag
> in hand. After a second, Ari tries to run after
> her, but Bennett stops her. Ari is left watching
> her sister disappear down the hallway.*

End of Play.

CANCEL QUEEN

*by Alexis Jacquelyn Smith, Amber Steigelfest,
and Leslie Ureña*

Overview
a 20-min satirical comedy
for 4 actors, 3 female, 1 male

Synopsis
Cancel Queen is a sharp, provocative play where three
women embody the shifting roles of accuser, accused,
and onlooker in the high-stakes arena of cancel culture.
With wit and intensity, it challenges the audience to
question who truly holds the blame when judgment
goes viral.

Characters

ERNABETH (ERNA)   – female, 20s, white,
                       the worst
MARIANA (MARI)   – female, 20s, Latina,
                       publicity queen
ALBERTINE (ALBIE)   – 20s, bi-racial black and
                       white woman
NATE HUDSON   – male, 30s, the actual worst

Setting
New York City 2022, directly following the pandemic

Notes

It is our deepest hope that anyone who performs
Cancel Queen understands that the internet is a deeply
frustrating and hilarious place.
Props: Cocaine, Phones, Crazy Wardrobe, Snacks, Pen,
Contract, Room Spray.
Sound: GMA Intro, Fart Cues.
Lighting: Spotlights on Mari during her waves to the
audience.

Original Premiere

Cancel Queen premiered on June 15th, 2024, at the
2024 Extravaganza One Act Fest, directed by
Wolfgang Bodison.

Original Cast

ERNABETH (ERNA)   – Amber Steigelfest
MARIANA (MARI)   – Leslie Ureña
ALBERTINE (ALBIE) – Alexis Jacquelyn Smith
NATE HUDSON   – Will Hart

Performance Rights

This play may not be performed, reproduced, or
adapted without written permission from the author. To
request performance rights, please contact:
Amber Steigelfest, ambersteigelfest@gmail.com

Scene 1

Lights up on ERNA singing and dancing around the green room of GMA with a bottle of champagne in her hand. Makeup litters the vanity table. The coffee table and bar are covered in snacks and a cheese board. MARI bursts through the door.

MARI. I cannot believe we're here on Good Morning Fucking Amercia!

ERNA. Thanks to you, Mamacita!

MARI. And all thanks to you because you canceled that redneck singing racist pedophile Nate Hudson.

ERNA. Well, *you* took me from TikTok to the top!

MARI. All because *YOU* found out that song he sang was actually about his cousin.

ERNA. I remember like it was just yesterday.

ERNA has her hand on MARI. LIGHTS FADE with dream music. Spotlight on NATE.

NATE. Hello Texas! My gun-lovin' state. I love playing here for you all. I can just feel the FREEDOM in this crowd. Speaking of freedom, I got a present for y'all. My new song, never before seen, goes out to one special lady tonight. A one, two, three.

NATE starts singing.

NATE. My girl's sweet / Young and sweet/ Just
        sixteen/ So cute so sweet/ Pretty / Like a bald
        eagle / Flying in the sky / With old glory beside
        it

ERNA storms the stage.

ERNA. Nate Hudson is a pedophile!
NATE. WHAT?
ERNA. He's singing about his 16-year-old cousin
        Renee!
NATE. What? I -

*ERNA holds up a picture of NATE with an X
and PEDOPHILE on it. He continues to sing,
improvising.*

NATE. *(singing)* You can't cancel love / So what she's
        my cousin? You can't butt in-

The crowd boos!

ERNA. I actually can put my fat ass wherever I want.
NATE. *(singing)* Free / We're white and free / Cancel
        queen, internet Nazi
ERNA. I'm literally Jewish.

NATE. Damnit! Free /You can't fuck with me/ Keep
      coming for me /And you'll see…
ERNA. Is that a threat?!

NATE freaks out. The crowd continues to boo.

NATE. Fuck this. I love my cousin Renee like I love
      the USA. I'm not ashamed. Don't let these
      fuckin'libtards boss you around. And if they
      do, fight back. That's why we have the Second
      Amendment-

*LIGHTS FADE. Back up to ERNA and MARI in
the green room.*

MARI. Yeah, I remember. It's like you stole all his
      followers.
ERNA. He's a nobody now.
MARI. You know, you somehow made cancel culture
      a family-friendly affair.
MARI & ERNA: *WE* are the Queens of Cancel
      Culture.
ERNA. Oh! Do you have any *cocaina* on you,
      señorita?
MARI. For sure, *mi jefacita.* Oh wait, do you want any
      Lactaid in this for all the cheese you've been
      eating?

ERNA snorts coke off of MARI's wrist.

ERNA. No, I'm too powerful. Nothing can hurt me
     now. Not even cheese.
MARI. Okay, but lay off a little, okay? I need you
     focused. We've been waiting for this GMA
     segment to expose Barone Brown, an actual
     political figure. This is really going to launch
     your career and mine!

     *MARI steps forward into the spotlight like she's
     receiving unheard applause.*

ERNA. Hello? Mari?

     *MARI snaps out of it and returns to Erna's
     side.*

ERNA. The look on their faces when they find out
     Barone Brown, beloved internet activist for the
     Black Lives Matter movement, is actually a
     RAGING transphobe. They're gonna be pissed!

     *ERNA reveals a "CANCEL BARONE THE
     TRANSPHOBE" sign of Barone Brown.*

MARI. *SHHHHH!*
ERNA. Sorry! I'm just so excited. Everyone got so
     mad at me because I wouldn't go to protests in
     2020 because of my weak immune system, and
     now one of the leaders of Black Lives Matter

turns out to be a total transphobe. All I'm saying is, BLM and *Harry Potter* are out.

MARI. Word. It really sucks when people in power abuse it.

MARI takes ERNA to the vanity and starts to get her ready.

ERNA. Ugh, what do you think people will say about me for canceling a black man? You know how *they* get.

MARI. I'm your PR manager. Do you trust me or not?

ERNA. Duh. I literally signed over my whole brand to you in exchange for you doing all the research.

MARI. Exactly. You might get a little heat but it's because you'll be getting so much more praise. All press is good press. Right?

ERNA. Right! Besides, being a woman is more of a minority than being any race of man. We can all agree on that.

MARI grabs the powder and starts blotting Erna's face.

MARI. Yup. After five years, and crushing all the mediocre guys in the office, the men at the firm finally agreed that once you hit one million followers, they'll make me a partner.

MARI steps into the spotlight again.

ERNA. Mari! Focus!!!
MARI. RIGHT!

KNOCK at the door.

ERNA. Thank you, five.

The door opens. ALBIE enters. ERNA doesn't turn around.

ALBIE. Cancel Queen's dressing room?
MARI. This is my client's dressing room. Who are you?
ALBIE. I'm her cousin. Albertine Jackson. But you can call me Albie.

ERNA chokes on a grape.

MARI. No way! Erna, why were you so worried about getting canceled? You have a multiracial family. You're fine. We need to get this on IG because the people need to know. This is perfect! Let's get a little behind-the-scenes action. We need pics!

MARI grabs ALBIE and shoves her towards ERNA. They look at each other in confusion.

MARI. C'mon, give Charlie's Angels. Okay, cute, #blackfamilymatters. Okay, Albie now throw your arm around her!

ALBIE half chokes ERNA.

ERNA. (*through clenched teeth*) What are you doing here?
ALBIE. I'm here to support my liberal, understanding, tolerant cousin that's canceling all the horrible people in the world!
MARI. Posting!
ALBIE. Wow… and you have some color on your team. You really are woke, huh!

Phone rings.

MARI. It's the Partners. I have to take this. DON'T go anywhere. We need more content!

MARI exits. ALBIE releases ERNA, who half falls to the ground.

ERNA. OMG, so good to see you.
ALBIE. Cut the bullshit. This whole thing you're doing is a sham!
ERNA. What? Holding people accountable is a sham? You obviously have no idea about fighting for human rights.

ALBIE. Are you serious?

ERNA. Of course I am! What is this? What is going on? How are you even here?

ALBIE. I'm Barone Brown's assistant. I heard your voice down the hall.

ERNA. What a small fucking world. I have an assistant and you *are* an assistant.

ALBIE. Alright, bitch, do you even remember the last time we saw each other?

ERNA. Yeah, I saw you at a frat house bonfire and the rest was a mystery.

ALBIE. Let's talk about that bonfire, huh? You were a real treat that night.

Silence.

ERNA. Albertine, I was drunk. I know I get a little crazy but I couldn't have possibly done anything to warrant you cutting me out of your life and leaving me with those animals!

ALBIE. We'll let you be the judge of that.

Albertine whips out her phone.

We hear the voice of a different girl shouting "ERNABETH LIKES BLACK DICK", followed by a younger Ernabeth shouting back "I DO NOT! I WOULD NEVER SUCK A BLACK DICK THAT'S DISGUSTING!"

*Albertine turns off the video and looks
pointedly at Erna.*

ERNA. Albie, I ….I would never say something like
    that now.
ALBIE. But you did.
ERNA. Can you just… delete it?
ALBIE. How about, no.
ERNA. That's why you stopped talking to me? I was a
    kid.
ALBIE. A racist kid. And a terrible cousin. How did
    you think it made me feel to hear that?
ERNA. Well, why did you ditch me? Why not say
    something at the time? Teach me.

*ERNA jumps for ALBIEs phone. ALBIE
snatches it away and hits ERNA'S hands away.*

ALBIE. It's not my job to teach you about being racist.
    Like the hypocritical shit you're doing right
    now.
ERNA. What are you trying to say? Because I am a
    white woman, I can't stand against racism,
    homophobia, misogyny, and Republicanism?
    Honestly… it's coming off as reverse racist
    here, if you ask me. What would Martin think?
ALBIE. Martin?
ERNA. Luther.
ALBIE. I don't know, would you suck his dick?

ERNA. NO! EW! No I mean… not no because he's black, but no because he's not my type. I would suck Michael B. Jordan's dick!

ALBIE. Every white woman would suck Michael B. Jordan's dick. You have no right to be canceling anyone, *Ernabeth*. And once I post this video, everyone will know that!

ERNA. Please don't post the video! You'll ruin my life! You'll cancel me!

ALBIE. Then get out of here… and leave Barone alone.

ERNA. Barone? You're going to cancel your family, your blood, over some guy?

ALBIE. He's not some guy, he's a civil rights activist!

ERNA. He is transphobic!

ALBIE. That's besides the point!

ERNA. Wow… and you call yourself a liberal.

ALBIE. You're a WHITE WOMAN canceling a BLACK MAN!

ERNA screams Britney Spears style and lunges for ALBIE.

ALBIE. You take one more step, and I'll expose your racist ass--

MARI enters.

MARI. What the fuck is going on?

ALBIE. You two are going to walk away and let
     Barone have his segment before I expose
     Ernabeth as a racist.

MARI. Ernabeth, a white woman? Racist? Nooo.

ERNA. I'm not racist!

ALBIE. She was!

ERNA. But not anymore!

ALBIE. She's canceling a black man!

MARI. For being transphobic! Look. What can we do
     to make this go away?

ALBIE. Leave! Now! Or the video gets uploaded!

MARI. Video? There's footage?! *ERNA*!

ALBIE. Out you all go.

MARI. That's not an option. This is the biggest
     moment of her career.

ERNA. I'll pay you. Anything.

ALBIE. It's not about money.

ERNA. Do you want to be famous? We can do
     collabs? I'll make reparations.

MARI. I'll write the contracts!

ALBIE. No. It's about Barone, I want you to leave him
     alone.

ERNA. Albie, black people can be bad too. Look at
     OJ.

     ALBIE gives MARI a look. MARI pulls ERNA
     away.

MARI. Why do you care about him so much? Do you
      know him?
ALBIE. I'm his assistant.
MARI. You can be my assistant!
ALBIE. And he's my fiance!
MARI. Ohh, you could be my *puta*... actually, never
      mind.
ERNA. Your what?! Wait--was I not going to be
      invited to the wedding? I know we're estranged
      but we once talked about being each other's
      maids of honor--
MARI. Cancel Queen, focus!
ERNA. Right! Albie, you can't marry a transphobe!
      Please, I thought this was about being better
      people. Albie, please. Please, Albie, I'm not a
      transphobe and he is, pick me over him.

      ERNA is on the ground begging.

MARI. Oh, get up!

      *MARI goes to pull ERNA up. ERNA lets out a
      giant fart. The girls begin to gag from the
      smell.*

MARI. Aw shit, I told you about that Lactaid.
ALBIE. You guys are so superficial! Just stay in your
      lane and keep canceling MAGA assholes like

Nate Hudson and leave respectable people like Barone alone.

MARI. He said "Who cares about guys who want to wear dresses when there are black people getting killed in the street?" That's horrible!

ALBIE. So is her fucking ass! Get her out of here!

MARI. *(to ERNA)* I told you about that damn Lactaid!

ERNA. THE STRESS IS TRIGGERING ME! I DIDN'T PLAN ON BEING THIS STRESSED!

ALBIE. Get out!!!

ERNA runs off. ALBIE runs to the snack table to stuff food in her mouth. MARI sprays room spray.

ALBIE. It's in my mouth! It's in my mouth!

MARI. Listen, POC to POC... woman to woman, she's doing us a favor, no? For the most part?

ALBIE. No, she's not! She has used our people's struggles for likes and retweets and now she's going to destabilize a political movement for her own 15 minutes of fame? And you're just letting it happen!

MARI. I am!

ALBIE. How can you go along with this?

MARI. Because Albie, people like us don't get here very often. I'm a first-generation Latina with immigrant parents. Opportunities like this one are not written for us. I had to work my ass off for this opportunity as a PR assistant. Yet you think you're high and mighty, ruining my client because she said something fucked up in the past? If you post this, I'll lose my job and everything that I've worked hard for. So tell me, what's the difference between her and you?

ALBIE. I feel for you, I really do. But I can't let this happen to him. He deserves better. You both do.

MARI. You think I don't know that? In this business, we gotta tolerate a lot of shit from people like her to make it. If I took on only respectable clients, with respectable problems, I wouldn't make a dollar. The world runs on chaos, Albie. Your cousin is the center of that right now. Getting rid of her doesn't just get rid of the chaos, it just changes the source of it. So please, have some sympathy for me, and just go.

ALBIE. I can't. I won't.

MARI. Look, nothing you do here is going to make a difference. The story is getting run regardless. The word is already out. I can assure you this is the best thing for Barone's career.

ALBIE. What on earth are you talking about?

MARI. *Te lo explico en español!*

ALBIE. Uhhhh… Sorry, I'm only level one Duolingo…

MARI. Okay, then never mind! Look, Barone is a
     nobody to anybody that doesn't directly follow
     him. He gets exposed on GMA, and I assure
     you he can flip the script on this White Karen
     and gain traction. We'll go from online activist
     to a seat in the senate.

ALBIE. I don't know.

MARI. If you loved him, you'd let this happen.

ALBIE. That's crazy.

MARI. People love an underdog. Look, I'm about as
     done with this bitch as you are and I've only
     known her a few months. You and Barone
     interest me. Imagine this: You let this happen,
     and I hook Barone up with a story on GMA
     defending himself against Erna… showing he's
     a changed man. A man who champions trans
     rights and black rights! He becomes an icon
     and Erna is history. I take you both on as
     clients and boom: A power couple… the new
     Obamas.

ALBIE. I want that…

MARI. But only if you let this happen. After this,
     she'll hit her 1 million followers, I'll get my
     promotion, ditch her, and rep you guys, okay?
     I'll go get the paperwork right now. You just…
     stay right here.

ERNA comes back. The women hush.

ERNA. Please don't let anyone use that toilet… I
    cannot let that dump get leaked.
MARI: *Ya para de causar problemas, nomas piensas*
    en ti y yo aca como pendeja haciendo negocios
    para arreglarte todo. Ya casi me voy, y te voy a
    dejar sin nada-
ERNA: *(in between Mari's rant)* Mari, you know that I
    don't *espeak Espanish-*
MARI: *Me llamo Mari!!! Y porque no hablan*
    español!?

    MARI exits. ERNA looks at ALBIE pathetically,
    hands behind her back.

ERNA. Albie… You're right. I suck.
ALBIE. I know you do. You don't have to manipulate
    me.
ERNA. I'm not. Albie, while I was sitting on the toilet
    I thought about how hard everything must have
    been for you. I mean all the things our grandma
    used to say, with me clearly being the favorite.
    All the things I used to repeat. I've been
    running from that person, so I don't blame you
    for running from that version of me too. I
    actually think I ended up on the toilet because
    of how anxious it makes me that I hurt you.

    ERNA begins to reach towards ALBIE. We see
    her hands are covered in excrement.

ERNA. I don't know if you know this, but your bowels are linked to your brain. I feel so sick just thinking about it, I couldn't imagine how you walked through life dealing with insensitivity from your own family.

ALBIE. I'm not going to say it's okay but -- wait. Is that shit on your hands?

ERNA. I have a lot of shit to deal with all the time. But yes, currently I have shit on my hands. I need to go use a different bathroom that has soap, but I had to talk to you immediately.

ALBIE. *(gagging)* Erna, please go wash your fucking hands!

ERNA. Believe it or not, I started doing this because I felt like I was making a difference. That by canceling people, I was creating a better narrative. But then everyone liked what I was doing so much, I started to do it for their attention rather than justice. I just chased the validation. All I'm trying to say is that I'm sorry, Albie. Really.

ALBIE. Okay! Okay!

ERNA. You know what, Albie. I'm going to be a good person. Starting right now. I'm not going on anymore. GMA is so pre-TikTok anyway. I'm not going on.

MARI enters.

MARI. Like fuck you're not. Albie, I thought we
     agreed you wanted Erna to have the moment
     she deserves for all her hard work?

*Out of ERNA's view, MARI starts to rip a
contract but ALBIE motions her not to. MARI
puts it behind her back.*

ALBIE. Well-
ERNA. Honestly, Taylor Swift rose from the ashes. I
     can too. I'm not gonna ruin your relationship.
MARI. What about your career, Erna, and mine?
ERNA. What about Barone's career? I'm not
     backstabbing my cousin. You can see yourself
     out.
MARI. You can see yourself out the fuck on stage!
ERNA. Excuse me?!

ERNA steps up to MARI.

ALBIE. Erna! Stop. You were right in canceling
     Barone.
ERNA. I was?
ALBIE. Barone's transphobia is deplorable behavior. It
     shouldn't go unchecked.
MARI. Exactly.

*MARI flips to the signature page. ALBIE
quickly signs it behind ERNA's back.*

ALBIE. I didn't see it until I had a very…enlightening
    conversation with Mari. But I think it's only
    fair that you go on stage and cancel him.
    Transphobia is never right, regardless of who it
    is coming from.
ERNA. Albie…
ALBIE. Justice is justice.

ERNA considers. MARI grows impatient.

MARI. I also own your brand. I own your image. Your
    car. Your house--

ALBIE steps in between MARI and ERNA.

ALBIE. What she means is! You have a lot to lose. So
    go on, do your thing.
ERNA. Okay. Only because of you, cuzzo.

*ERNA points at ALBIE. MARI notices her
    hands.*

MARI. Fuck, what's on your hands?
ERNA. There wasn't any soap in the bathroom.
MARI. *Pinche Mierda.*

MARI pulls baby wipes out.

MARI. Here.

ERNA. Thank you, Mari. I'm glad we're all on the same team again. Women unite! We're really the marginalized--

MARI gets cocaine from pocket ready.

ALBIE. Erna. Please. Sometimes the best thing you can do to save the world is shut the fuck up.

ERNA snorts cocaine from MARI's hand.

ERNA. Heard and felt.
MARI. Alright, you're on. You know what to do. Just don't embarrass either of us out there, okay?

ERNA jumps up and down like a fighter, goes to the door. MARI and ALBIE high five. ERNA opens it... to reveal NATE HUDSON with a shotgun.

NATE. FUCK YOU CANCEL QUEEN!

NATE shoots ERNA. The women pause for a second, then scream. NATE steps over ERNA's body and points the gun at MARI.

MARI. Please! No!
NATE. She ruined my life and you helped her.

NATE inches toward MARI with the gun.

MARI. No. Nate. You don't understand-

NATE cocks the shotgun.

MARI. I CAN MAKE YOU A STAR! The next big influencer/mass shooter. Except this time, you won't be forgotten like the rest of them. I'm talking about book deals, documentaries, and films. With the right lawyer, I can even get you out of this. I know a guy! JUST DON'T SHOOT ME!
MARI cowers.

NATE. I can't be an influencer mass shooter only having killed one person.

MARI looks to ALBIE. NATE fires at ALBIE. BLACKOUT.

End of Play.

COLD BLOODED

by Sonny Schnapf, Will Hart, and Evan Adams

Overview
a 15-minute drama
for 5 actors, 4 male, 1 female

Synopsis
A ruthless, old West gunslinger must confront his life
of crime in one haunting night of rage, regret, and
possible redemption.

Characters
SID NICHOLS   – male, 30's- 40's
KIT BARRON   – male, 20's-30's
THOMAS NICHOLS   – male, 20's, Sid's brother
SARAH NICHOLS   – female, 20's, Thomas's
                                           wife
GARRETT T. JOHNSTON – male, 20's-50's, lawyer

Setting
The Nichols' family ranch, 1875.

Notes
There are time jumps between scenes. Decoration and
condition of the ranch should reflect the change in
ownership between Thomas and Sid.

Original Premiere
Cold Blooded premiered on June 8th, 2024, at the 2024
Extravaganza One Act Fest, directed by Wolfgang
Bodison.

Original Cast

SID NICHOLS	– Will Hart
KIT BARRON	– Sonny Schnapf
THOMAS NICHOLS	– Evan Adams
SARAH NICHOLS	– Natalia
Montgomery	
GARRETT T. JOHNSTON	– Eric Dion Kubal

Performance Rights

This play may not be performed, reproduced, or adapted without written permission from the author. To request performance rights, please contact Sonny Schnapf at sonnyschnapf1@gmail.com.

Will Hart and Sonny Schnapf,
photo by Grant Terzakis

Scene 1

The stage is dark. Spotlight on a dead body lying center stage. Kit Barron kneels over the body looting his pockets. Sid Nichols stands upstage in the shadows checking a pocket watch. He then shoots Kit and pockets the watch. Kit keels over, dead. Sid exits. Lights out.

Scene 2

Lights up on the interior of a ranch house. There is a desk downstage left, a dresser upstage center, a chair and a bookcase downstage right. A door upstage left leads outside while a door upstage right leads to a bedroom. It looks poorly kept. A knocking and a voice comes from outside the upstage left door.

GARRETT. Mr. Nichols?! I need to speak with you.

Garrett knocks again. Sid enters from the bedroom, whiskey bottle in hand, buckling his gun belt.

GARRETT. Mr. Nichols?
SID. Hold your horses, damnit! I'm coming.
GARRETT. It really is quite urgent, sir.
SID. Yeah, yeah.

Sid reaches the door, but doesn't open it. He draws his revolver.

SID. Who is it?
GARRETT. Garett T. Johnston. Attorney at law. We
        have some business to discuss.
SID. Business? A little late in the evening for business,
        ain't it?
GARRETT. Well you haven't returned any of our
        telegrams, and this really is quite an urgent
        matter. Just spare me a moment of your time
        and I'll be on my way.

Beat.

SID. Fine! Just keep your hands where I can see 'em
        and don't try nothin'!
GARRETT. You have my word.

*Sid opens the door and Garrett walks in, hand
out to shake Sid's hand. Sid does not extend his
own. Sarah Nichols enters in a rush after
Garrett. She immediately moves toward Sid, but
Garrett intervenes. Sid grabs his bottle and
moves to the chair to sit down.*

SID. You again!? My god, you are one persistent
        female! Gotta hand it to ya. You had me fooled.
        And who are you, really? Her new boyfriend?
SARAH. You son of a bitch!
SID. Hey, now. That ain't very ladylike.

*Sarah moves toward Sid, as though she may hit
him. Garrett steps in between them.*

GARRETT. Please, Mrs. Nichols, let me handle this.

*Garrett guides Sarah away. He then turns to
address Sid.*

GARRETT. I'm just a lawyer sir. Handling the account
of your late brother on behalf of your sister-in-
law.

SID. What're you talking about?

SARAH. He's helping me get my house back, you
horse's ass!

SID. Watch that now!

SARAH. What? You gonna kill me just like you killed
Thomas?

GARRETT. Mrs. Nichols, please! She's still in
mourning.

SID. They never could prove what happened to poor
ol' Tom. Seems there weren't any witnesses.
I'm all torn up over it. It's only right I be the
one to take over the ranch. Seein' as how I'm
the last of the family.

SARAH. You're not the last of the family. I was Tom's
family, more than you ever were. He would
want me and Grace, his daughter, your niece to
have the ranch. You took everything from us!
You have no idea what it's been like. Some
nights we have nowhere to sleep. We go days
without food, and now Grace is getting sick.
This ranch isn't just our home; it's our
livelihood. Show some humanity.

GARRETT. Mrs. Nichols, please allow me to do my
job. You see, Mr. Nichols, the ownership of this
ranch is exactly what's in dispute. Now we
hope to handle this amicably, but if need be we
can take it to the courts.

SID. The courts, huh? Well you tell Ol' Judge Brown Sid Nichols sends his regards, then we'll see what your courts are good for.

GARRETT. Now, we're not looking for a fight here. But if you force our hand, we can go to the sheriff.

SID. You can tell that little bitch hiding behind that big ol' badge that if he wants to take what's mine, he can come on and try. Now it's getting late, I'm tired. *(He rises.)* Y'all best be on your way.

Garrett backs up, but doesn't leave. Sarah stands firm.

GARRETT. Well… um, I see, if you would just… You see we can certainly come to some type of—

SID. LEAVE!

Garrett pivots on his heel and swiftly walks out the door.

GARRETT. I see, well it's late. We'll be in touch, good night!

Sarah and Sid remain. She turns and approaches him.

SARAH. The sins of your past will haunt you, Sid Nichols. Monsters like you always get their due.

She walks out.

SID. Monsters? Nah, just a man.

He grabs his bottle of whiskey and sits down at his desk. He takes another pull from the bottle, picks up the guitar that is resting on the wall next to him and plays the opening phrase of "Red River Valley." The lights fade to black until a single spot illuminates Sid. Lights go completely black.

Scene 3

A loud ticking sound comes on in the dark. The single spot over Sid returns, who is now asleep in his chair, hat tipped down over his eyes. There is a lightning flash and a loud bang of thunder. He awakens with a jolt. Sid begins searching the room for the source of the ticking. Rain and thunder can be heard outside.

SID. Where's that watch?

The ticking suddenly stops. Sid turns and draws his revolver.

SID. Who's there?

Another bang of thunder as Kit Barron approaches from the darkness. Sid points the gun at him.

KIT. Long time no see, big man.
SID. Kit… what the hell!?
KIT. Place is fallin' apart. I assume you've taken over around here?

Lights rise on the rest of the stage.

SID. You're dead.
KIT. Course I am. You shot me in the head!
SID. What is this?
KIT. I'm here for you, Sid.

Sid fires two shots. Kit is unharmed.

KIT. Ohhhh, you can put down the gun, ya know.
SID. No, this is a goddamn nightmare of some kind!

Sid runs for the front door. It is locked.

KIT. Ain't no nightmare, Sid. Your soul needs savin'.
SID. I must be losing my damn mind.
KIT. You lost it a long time ago.

Sid runs to the bedroom door. It too is locked.

KIT. You ain't changed one bit, Sid Nichols. Where ya'
think you're goin? You can't run no more. Time
to account for the past, time to account for what
you've done!

*Sid ebbs towards the dresser, begins
rummaging.*

SID. So what, you lookin' for an apology? You're no
angel. You killed a man for that jacket,
remember?
KIT. Ain't no apology gonna set me free. And you're
right, Sid, I was too naive to understand then,

but now, I see. I didn't get a chance to change
while I was still livin', but you do.
SID. What, you here for redemption?
KIT. Something like that…

Sid whips out a Bible, presenting it to Kit.

KIT. Oh, that ain't gonna save you.

*Defeated, Sid puts the Bible back, kicks the
drawer shut.*

KIT. Used to think I'd find something bigger than
myself out here…

*As Kit talks, Sid dismissively walks toward his
desk.*

KIT. All I found was you. I'm damned for what I did in
life. What we did.
SID. Enough with the lecture!

*Sid turns and rushes Kit. Thunder crashes and
lightning strikes. Sid falls to his knees frozen in
place, held by something supernatural. Kit
circles him as he speaks.*

KIT. This ain't no game, Sid! Frank, Bill, Woods,
Luke, me, poor ol' Tom! All them boys was
livin' life. We all believed we were fighting for
something bigger than ourselves, fighting
alongside you! That was a lie! *(Beat)* You
obviously don't remember that day like I do.
You need to see again!

Kit exits. Sid is frozen in place.

Scene 4

Months earlier. The house is in better condition. Tom enters and sits down stage left. Lights up on him unhooking his leg brace. Sid stands.

SID. I need that will!
TOM. Yeah, I figured you was here about the will, seein' as if you were here for the old man's funeral, you'd've been here months ago.
SID. You think I wanted to miss all this? Got caught up out there. Fightin' carried on some for me, but I'm here now.
TOM. Fightin'? War's been over for years. Who you been fighin'? Ghosts?

Tom rises, grabs a cane near the bookcase and begins to move about the house. Sid notices a gold chain hanging from Tom's pocket.

SID. Say, is that the old man's pocket watch ya got there?
TOM. Yeah, what's it to ya?
SID. You know that was supposed to be mine.
TOM. Yeah, well you burned that bridge, didn't ya? You left and never came back, got lost out there. He thought you was dead.
SID. I didn't get lost, Thomas. I did what I had to do. You ain't got a clue. You've sat on this ranch your whole life. Ya' know, you should be grateful it was me who went off to fight... Now

if you ain't gonna tell me where the will is, I'll find it myself…

Sid starts to look around.

TOM. Would you cut the shit, Sid! *(Beat)* Look, why don't you stick around for dinner. The girls will be back from town soon. It'd be nice for y'all to get to know each other.
SID. The girls?
TOM. Yeah, got a wife and daughter now. Startin' a family. And listen, if it's money ya need, you can work here. Lay your arms down and come home. Join the family.
SID. You don't understand, it ain't that simple.
TOM. It is that simple! Come on, I'm your brother, I wanna help. And lord knows I sure could use an extra set a' hands around here This could be OUR ranch.
SID. I don't think so. Where's the will?
TOM. Sid, stop, alright? It's not here, we all thought you were dead. He wrote you out of it.
SID. Don't lie to me, Thomas.
TOM. Ain't no lie, that's the truth, Sid. Don't be blinded by your greed!
SID. Damnit! Where is it?!

Sid puts his hand on the hilt of his revolver.

TOM. Are you threatening me?
SID. I need that will!

Sid unholsters his revolver.

TOM. So this is how it is then? You gonna show up
     here, after all this time and shoot me? I got a
     family now!

Sid points his revolver at Tom.

TOM. Sid, please, don't! You don't gotta do this!
SID. Where is it?!
TOM. It's at the bank in town, in dad's lockbox… He
     was right about you, you did get lost out there.
SID. If it's in his lockbox, I'll need a key. Where you
     keeping it?

*Tom doesn't answer. Sid cocks the hammer of
his revolver.*

SID. The key, Thomas!
TOM. It's in the bedroom. In the drawer of the
     nightstand.

*Sid walks to the bedroom. Tom stands and looks
out, away from the bedroom.*

TOM. You know, I'd lay awake at night as a kid,
     thinking about what I'd do, what I'd say if I
     saw you again. You ain't the man I remember.
     You're just a coward… You won't find
     anything in that will that'll lead you back from
     the darkness!

*Sid quickly returns, key in hand, while Tom is
mid-speech. Sid shoots him. Tom looks up at Sid
in shock. He falls to one knee. Tom extends a
hand to Sid, pleading for help. Sid approaches*

Tom and takes his pocket watch. Sid walks towards the front door. He pauses, then turns and draws his revolver, firing one last shot. Tom falls down dead.

SID. Some of us don't get to choose who we become!

Sid bangs on the front door. Kit enters.

KIT. Got what we need?
SID. Just about. Check his pockets. And grab that pocket watch, will ya?

Kit starts patting Tom's body down. Sid pulls the pocket watch back out, and opens it to admire his prize. He then draws his revolver.

KIT. Ain't no watch here, Sid…

Without looking, Sid points his gun at the back of Kit's head.

SID. I know.

Kit raises his head, a moment of realization. Sid shoots Kit in the head. Kit falls down dead. Sid turns to exit through the front door, but it is locked. Lights turn red. Ominous music rises. Ghostly whispers and screams can be heard. More lightning and thunder. Sid turns back around. Kit rises from the dead.

KIT. You see, this is who you are. This is the world
        you created. And hell awaits you if you don't
        change!
SID. No! This is just a goddamn nightmare!

Tom rises. Sid turns again to see.

SID. Get out of my head!

*Sid runs for the bedroom door. It's locked too.
Kit and Tom pursue in a zombie-like state.*

TOM. See what you've done! You killed the only
        family you had. Now you're damned.

*Sid runs to center stage when another crack of
thunder brings him to his knees.*

KIT. You're a dead man walking. If you keep carrying
        on like this, you'll be damned for an eternity.
        You'll wear the chains you forged in life, like I
        do!
SID. You don't scare me!
TOM. Pa always used to say "the wicked flee." He was
        talking about you!

Tom and Kit close in on either side of Sid.

SID. Go away, damnit!
KIT. You're on a one-way train to hell, Sid Nichols!
SID. I ain't afraid! I've already seen hell!
KIT. Oh, no you ain't, not the real thing at least. Here's
        what awaits you!

Kit and Tom thrust their hands toward Sid, his head jerks back, his eyes wide. The music becomes clamorous and terrifying. In one final moment, Sid sees hell and screams. The sound of a gun cocking and firing can be heard. Lights out.

Scene 5

Back to present time. The ticking fades in again. Spotlight on Sid, asleep at his desk. Hat pulled over his eyes, whiskey bottle right next to him. A crack of thunder. The ticking stops. Sid wakes from his slumber. He takes a moment and looks around. The nightmare is seemingly over. The rest of the lights come up. Sid pulls out his revolver and looks at it. He opens the drawer of the desk and throws it in there. As he goes to close it, he notices something. He reaches in and pulls out the pocket watch. He holds it up. One last crack of thunder. Lights out.

End of Play.

BABY ELLA

by Ashley Elsa White

Overview
a 10-minute drama
for 3 actors, 2 female and 1 male

Synopsis
A woman's plea for her husband to bond with their
baby becomes a confrontation with a secret that could
destroy their family forever.

Characters
ROSE   – female, early 30s, a new mother determined
            to repair her marriage
ERIC   – male, early 30s, kind and patient with his
            wife, a lawyer who buries himself in his work
            to avoid coping
ALICE   – female, early thirties-forties, Rose's
            caregiver

Setting
Eric's home office, morning.

Notes
The top of the play should be lighthearted. Rose is
excited about her idea of how to rekindle her
relationship with her husband. The main prop needed is
a realistic looking fake baby. Other props are a food
tray, picnic basket, computer, and books. The window
and blinds should be downstage center on the fourth
wall. Opening and closing the blinds are shown with a

light cue. The song opening the piece should be "Tearin' Up My Heart" by N'Sync. The song closing the piece should be "Fix You" by Coldplay.

Music Use Note
Licensees must secure permission for any copyrighted music or use only original music they own. All music clearances are the licensee's responsibility, and they agree to indemnify the copyright owners and licensing agent against any related claims.

Original Premiere
Baby Ella premiered on June 8th, 2024 at the 2024 Extravaganza One Act Fest, directed by Wolfgang Bodison.

Original Cast
ROSE   – Ashley Elsa White
ERIC   – Eric Dion Kubal
ALICE   – Annie Creech

Performance Rights
This play may not be performed, reproduced, or adapted without written permission from the author. To request performance rights, please contact Ashley Elsa White at ashleyelsa@hotmail.com.

Eric Dion Kubal and Ashley Elsa White,
photo by Grant Terzakis

Scene 1

Cue music, Tearin' Up My Heart by N'Sync. Lights up. We see a man in a home office working vigorously at his desk. He goes to the window and closes the blinds, before grabbing more books from the bookshelf. A woman enters abruptly, holding a baby and a tray of food.

ROSE. *(Excitedly)* Yoohoo!

ERIC. Hey, Sweetie.

ROSE. Somebody forgot to come down for lunch again.

ERIC. Oh right, it totally slipped my mind.

ROSE. Don't worry, I brought you a little snack.

ERIC. Thank you, Rose.

ROSE. Why don't you join us for a walk to the gardens? Like we used to do? I feel like Ella could use some sunshine today.

ERIC. I wish I could, but I need to finish preparing my case for tomorrow.

ROSE. But you've been working long hours all week… Surely a walk with us would be refreshing.

ERIC. That's a good point, Sweetheart, but my trial is really early tomorrow and every second counts right now.

ROSE. That's right. Every second does count. We're your family, Eric. Tomorrow is never promised.

We see this hits ERIC hard as he thinks about her words.

ROSE. Please, Eric. We don't even have to stay. Just a short walk to the garden and back is all I'm asking of you.

She hands the baby to Eric.

ERIC. I really wish I could, but I can't right now.
ROSE. We barely spend any quality time together anymore. And look, it's a beautiful day outside.

ROSE opens the curtains to let light flood the room.

ERIC. Rose, can we please not start this again.

Eric closes the curtains. Throughout the following lines, Rose straightens up the office, putting books on the shelves. Eric follows her and puts books back where he had them.

ROSE. I'm sorry. I wasn't trying to start anything.
ERIC. *(Growing aggravated)* You know how time consuming my job can be. This case is no different.
ROSE. Well, before Ella was born, you always had time to go for a walk.
ERIC. Before the baby was born, I wasn't working overtime either.
ROSE. I know. I'm sorry I'm not pulling my weight financially at the moment…
ERIC. It's not about that, Rose. Look, I can't go on a walk with you today, but maybe next week, after this case has wrapped up.

*He hands the baby back to Rose. She moves to
the center of the room, while he goes back to
his work. She looks at the baby and thinks
about what to say next before saying it.*

ROSE. *(Accusingly)* You always say that, though, you
     know.
ERIC. *(Dismissively)* I don't have time to deal with
     this right now. I need to finish my work.

*She turns to watch him, as anger starts to boil.
She waits until he looks up at her before
approaching and confronting him further. This
section of dialogue can overlap slightly.*

ROSE. You distanced yourself from us the moment
     Ella was born.
ERIC. I wish you could understand…
ROSE. What I understand is that you're burying
     yourself in your work in order to avoid
     spending time with us.
ERIC. That's not what I'm doing…
ROSE. That's exactly what you're doing, Eric! I know
     you're not attracted to me anymore. I gained
     weight during the pregnancy, and it took me too
     long to lose it, because of Ella's routine.
ERIC. No, Rose, that's not it at all and you've been a great
     mother.
ROSE. Then what is it? There's another woman, isn't
     there?
ERIC. *(warns her) Please* stop.
ROSE. That Alice lady you've hired. She's here awfully
     long hours every day. She even comes in on the

weekends. Be honest with me, are you having an affair with her?

ERIC. *(angrily)* No. Of course not! How can you even think that? *(softens)* There's only you. I promise.

There's a long pause as Rose takes in her husband's words.

ROSE. I'm sorry. I believe you. I just...I want things to go back to how they once were.

ERIC. That's exactly what I want too, Rose, but it's not that easy.

Eric recognizes how much Rose is hurting.

ERIC. You know what? You're right. We should go on that walk.

ROSE. Really? You mean it?

ERIC. I haven't been giving you enough of my time lately and I see now how much it's been affecting you. Let's put the baby in the crib and we can go on our walk.

ROSE. We can't just leave her here.

ERIC. Alice can watch over her.

ROSE. No. I don't trust that woman with my baby.

ERIC. Alice is perfectly capable. Please. Let's just be normal again for a day.

ROSE. Normal? What do you mean by normal?

ERIC. Come on, Rose. Let it be the two of us. Just for this walk.

ROSE. You've barely bonded with Ella. She needs to come with us.

He tries to take the baby from her.

ERIC. I can bond with her later. Give me the baby, please.
ROSE. No. Stop it! You're going to wake her up. Let go!
ERIC. Rose, it's okay. Just give her to me for a moment.
ROSE. Eric, stop. You're hurting her!
ERIC. She's fine, Rose. Now let go, so I can put her in the
      crib.

      They struggle over the baby until it drops to the
      floor, revealing it's just a doll.

ROSE. Look what you did! You made me drop her! Oh
      Ella, sweetie, please be okay.

      She kneels by the doll and slowly realizes what it
      is. She pulls down the zipper on the onesie to
      confirm her thoughts.

ROSE. No...no, this can't be...
ERIC. Rose?
ROSE. Eric? What's happening? This...This is just a doll!
ERIC. Oh, thank God, Rose! You're back!
ROSE. Back? Eric, where's Ella? Where's our baby?
ERIC. Honey. Ella didn't survive the birth. She was a
      stillborn.
ROSE. No...that can't be true.
ERIC. She's buried in the garden with the others.
ROSE. But I've been taking care of her every day...
ERIC. No you haven't. (*He points to the doll*) This...this
      doll is what you've been taking care of.
ROSE. How is that possible? I feed her and change her
      diapers.
ERIC. I know you do, but it's all pretend.
ROSE. (*insistent*) I've heard her giggle. I've comforted
      her when she's cried...

ERIC. Rose, please believe me, you've been losing your
         grip on reality.
ROSE. I rock her to sleep every night and sing her
         lullabies...
ERIC. You're wasting your time playing with a doll,
         instead of living your life with me!

She stares at him defeated, her reality shattered.

ROSE. I'm so confused, Eric.
ERIC. I know. I'm sorry.
ROSE. How could I have mistaken this doll for Ella?
ERIC. I don't know, Rose. The doctors said it would help
         you grieve the loss, but all it did was make things
         worse for you.
ROSE. Everything I must've put you through…I'm so
         sorry, Eric.
ERIC. *(Hugging her) It's* okay, Rose. It's not your fault.
         I'm just glad you're back.

*They live in that moment, until Eric feels ready to
move forward.*

ERIC. *(Excitedly)* You know what? We should go on that
         walk. We'll have a picnic like we used to do. Just
         let me pack up this food you prepared. Give me
         one second.

*Eric grabs the tray of food and turns his back to
Rose to pack the picnic basket upstage. The
audience sees Rose look back at the doll. After a
long moment, she moves towards the doll and
begins to redress and wrap it back up in the*

blanket. As she cradles the doll, Eric turns around. He stops in his tracks when he sees Rose.

ERIC. Rose, what are you doing?

Eric slowly approaches Rose as she comforts Ella.

ROSE. Shh, Ella, you're okay. Daddy didn't mean to… shh, don't cry. You're okay.

ROSE. *(turning towards Eric)* Isn't she beautiful, dear?

ERIC. *(pauses, staring at Rose at he wraps his arm around her waist)* Yes. Yes she is.

After a moment, Eric hopelessly walks back to his desk. Rose follows.

ROSE. Here. Give her a kiss, it will help her feel better.

Rose stretches out the baby towards Eric. He just stares at the doll.

ROSE. Eric. Give your daughter a kiss. It's important to show her you care.

Reluctantly, Eric kisses the baby on the forehead. She smiles at Eric.

ROSE. Don't worry, Dear. (*Looking at the baby*) She's still perfect. Not a scratch on her.

Eric smiles back sadly.

ERIC. That's great, Dear. I'm glad.

Rose goes off into her own world, putting all her attention back on the baby and begins to hum "If We Hold on Together" from The Land Before Time. After a moment, Eric quietly goes to the door and opens it.

ERIC. Nurse, can you come here please?

Alice, Rose's caregiver, enters the doorway.

ALICE. Is everything okay, Mr. Wallace?
ERIC. I had her back for a moment, Alice.
ALICE. That's good, Sir. That's progress. We shouldn't push her too hard, though. I need to give her her medication.
ERIC. Let me just say goodbye and she'll be out in a minute.
ALICE. Of course, Sir.
ERIC. Thank you.

Alice steps back into the hallway to allow privacy as Eric turns his attention back to Rose, who is still in her own world humming. He approaches her. As they talk to each other, Eric should be facing towards the direction of the desk, while Rose is facing the direction of the door.

ERIC. *(interrupting her)*. Hey, Sweetie. It's time for me to get back to work now. Thank you for stopping by. It really brightened my day.
ROSE. Of course. I'm glad you were able to take a little break for us.
ERIC. Always.

*Rose heads towards the door. Eric stays facing
away from her. He says his line before she opens
the door.*

ERIC. I love you, Sweetheart.
ROSE. *(turns and smiles at Eric)* I love you too, Dear.

*Rose turns to open the door. Cue music, Fix You
by Coldplay. Rose exits. Alice watches Eric
sympathetically for a moment before she closes
the door. He remains still, taking in everything
that just happened. Then slowly goes back to
work. Lights fade.*

End of Play.

BREAKING THE LINE

by Erin Hadfield

Overview
a 45-60 minutes drama
for 3 actors; 1 female, 1 male, and 1 any gender

Synopsis
Breaking the Line is a grisly one act drama, that
unravels a twisted tale instigated by a devastating loss.
A loss that forced Lily to come face to face with her
worst nightmare; one of the killers she hunts, making
her family, the hunted. As she is pulled in all
directions, Lily must battle between the duty to her
badge or crossing the line she swore she never would,
to avenge her daughter's heinous murder.

Characters
LILY O'BRIEN   – female, mid 30's, FBI Agent
SAMMI O'BRIEN   – female, mid 30's, Lily's wife
CAIN / THE MAN   – male, 40's, disheveled looking,
                              can be Irish

Setting
Present day, Las Vegas. The O'Brien's home splits the
stage; a living room on one side, and kitchen on the
other. A large kitchen table sits center stage; the main
action surrounds the table. Two exits, one for the other
areas of house, and one for the main door of house.

Notes
Sammi can be played by any gender; lines should be
adjusted accordingly.
As the play opens with Sammi and Lily at the table,
Cain is hovering in the back, like an image of his
presence in Lily's mind. A red light also hovers, and
turns off when he exits. He exits after Lily's line,
"Sammi, I can't do this."
Lily is coming home from work in Scene 2, so she
should be wearing her shield and gun with her hair tied
up; also carrying in groceries. A different look from
Scene 1 and Scene 3. Cain should be wearing Sammi's
apron and their coat should be strewn over the couch.
There should also be family photos of Lily, Sammi,
and their daughter Pacey.
There are some smaller stunts involved.

Original Premiere
Breaking the Line premiered on June 8, 2024, at the
2024 Extravaganza One Act Fest. The production was
directed by Wolfgang Bodison. The set design was by
Erin Hadfield and Wolfgang Bodison.

Original Cast
LILY O'BRIEN   – Erin Hadfield
SAMMI O'BRIEN – Mina Quarterman
CAIN / THE MAN – Eric Charles Jorgenson

Performance Rights
This play may not be performed, reproduced, or
adapted without written permission from the author. To
request performance rights, please contact E. Hadfield,
BreakingTheLineOfficial@gmail.com

Eric Charles Jorgenson, Erin Hadfield, and Mina Quarterman,
photo by Grant Terzakis

Scene 1

Lights up onto the O'Brien's home. LILY, mid-thirties, and SAMMI, mid-thirties. Lily is a serious no nonsense very special agent with the FBI. She is driven, focused, witty, and out spoken. Sammi is quietly reserved, highly intelligent, a thinker. She is usually abnormally kind and wears her heart on her sleeve; despite being a lawyer for the NSA. Lily and Sammi are married. They sit picking at their dinners on either side of a nicely decorated dining table. Neither eating, each occasionally glancing at the other wanting to speak, but their gazes never meet at the same time. The tension palatable and the silence is deafening.

The heat of the Vegas evening sun seeps in through the windows past the cool breeze of the air conditioner, causing increased tension to envelop the room. After some time, Sammi stands up and begins clearing the table. She scrapes the food into the garbage, as Lily stares off in the distance contemplating what to say next. Cain hovers in the background near the front door, occasionally Lily looks up at him and tries to shake off the thoughts. A red light encapsulates them until he leaves. As Sammi comes back to grab more dishes, Lily finally finds the words.

LILY. I am a federal agent with the FBI. I don't have the luxury of breaking the law when I see fit.

Sammi continues clearing table and doing dishes.

SAMMI. And what about defending our daughter's memory?

Lily takes hold of Sammi's arm gently to stop her.

LILY. Murder is not defending her memory Sam. Don't glamorize the fact that what you want is deep seeded revenge for what he did to her.

Sammi pulls away and keeps cleaning.

SAMMI. Yes! Yes, you're right Lily, and what is wrong with that?

LILY. Because I am a federal agent with the FBI. This revenge scenario won't end well.

SAMMI. Maybe it will save another kid from being a victim to Cain. Or maybe it will stifle this voice in my head that blames myself for letting him take her, to failing you both—

Lily stands up and takes hold of Sammi.

Lily. –You weren't the one to fail us…

Sammi pulls away but stays squared off with Lily.

SAMMI. Maybe it will stop this excruciating pain inside me.

*Sammi walks back over to the kitchen and
starts cleaning the counter faced toward
audience and away from Lily.*

LILY. And the fact that it could destroy us, that means
     nothing. If you cross the line of killing
     someone through the kind of revenge you are
     talking about, when you've never taken a life
     before it will change you Sam; you'll lose who
     you are.
SAMMI. I already lost who I was Lily. We both did.
LILY. That's why we have to investigate. Find new
     evidence to link the chain, which has to exist.
     We will bring him down Sam, you just have to
     have faith in my team now. It's all we can do.
SAMMI. It's not the only thing. Together we can find a
     way to do it and not get caught.
LILY. Who the hell do you think they are going to
     suspect first. We wouldn't get away with SHIT!
SAMMI. Exactly why I need you. You know how they
     think.

*Lily has taken Sammi's spot by the counter,
though she is turned away from the audience
facing Sammi. Over Sammi's shoulder, by the
front door, still stands Cain in the red hue,
which now takes over all of them. As Lily
pauses with heavy conflict, she stares past
Sammi at Cain; who now turns and stares
directly at Lily with a shit eating sinister grin.*

LILY. I can't do this.

*Cain gives one last I gotcha look, and exits.
The red light fades. Sammi pauses briefly as he
exits then continues.*

SAMMI. You mean you won't. Lily, if you don't do
        this with me, I'll do it myself and then without
        your help, I will probably get caught and go to
        jail for life; unless of course you protect me.
LILY. Wow, really. That's the wagon you want to hitch
        your trailer to. I either help you murder and
        torture a man —

Sammi interrupts-

SAMMI. He is not a man, he is a monster.

Lily continues on-

LILY. – Or I am now responsible for you going to
        prison. Nice, real nice. *(She pauses)* How dare
        you put this on me.
SAMMI. Lily please! I am begging you. I am sorry for
        doing it like this, but I don't know how else to
        convince you; I need your help. Please Lily,
        please…for Pacey.
LILY. I am trying to do what is right for her. Do you
        know how hard it is just to breathe, let alone be
        made to feel guilty because I don't want to
        throw the rest of our lives away.
SAMMI. You think it's not impossible for me to
        breathe too.
LILY. I am sorry. And I do get it more than I may
        show, but you have always been the voice of
        moral reason in this family, never wavering on

doing what is right. I need you to remember
that feeling.

SAMMI. That part of me is gone Lily, and I don't
know if I can ever go back to who I was before.

LILY. After he is brought in legally which will happen
– we will watch him fry. My team will not rest
til' they find the proof we need; he will fuck up
again.

SAMMI. Lily, you have been obsessively chasing this
man for years. Maybe if you two didn't have
this fucked up cat and mouse game, he
wouldn't have left her for you like a damn
present, and our daughter might still be alive.

*Lily looks like she has been gutted. Sammi
instantly regretful. Weighted silence settles
between them.*

LILY. You're right…Maybe if I had been quicker,
smarter, or as good of an agent as they think I
am, or a stay- at-home mom, then she would
still be alive. That's what you're really saying.

SAMMI. I didn't mean to…I know it wasn't your fault.
Her death is on both us, and —

LILY. — But she was not left for you. It's all a part of
his game. He did this to punish me, so yeah this
is my fault, and I will never forgive myself.
And that's why I won't let you do this.

SAMMI. I am sorry but the law has had too many
chances. I used my contacts at NSA to find his
location —

LILY. — Are you kidding me!?! Using your contacts at
NSA, you think we are not going to be linked
to Cain now?

Pause. Sammi upsets starts goes to the "bedroom" off stage and comes back with a bag. And throughout this next dialogue packs various weaponry, rope, duct tape, blow torch, etc.. Lily continually tries to stop her.

LILY. If we do this, if I attempt to go too far beyond the law, like you are asking me to do; I will lose the only two things I have left…my badge and you.

SAMMI. You won't lose me.

LILY. If we do this Sam, I will.

SAMMI. We can do this, together.

LILY. Sammi! You're still not listening to a thing I said. If you do this, if you are not able to let the law handle bringing Cain down and instead become a killer - something you are not and never have been…then you leave me no choice.

SAMMI. What does that mean. You'd turn me in?

LILY. Never.

Sammi takes this as good and takes the bag to leave.

LILY. What it means is, if you do this, then you leave me no choice but to…to take some time away. I refuse to sit back and watch you obliterate our lives because you are so blind with payback.

Sammi is jolted, and heavily conflicted. She too can't leave all she has left.

SAMMI. Lily, you can't leave.

LILY. Then you need to stop, babe.

Sammi pauses.

SAMMI. I'm not sure I can. I believe what I want to do
    is right.
LILY. It won't give you the satisfaction you think it
    will. Instead you will become even more
    hallow than you are now. Revenge is for the
    living, not for the dead. So, go talk to a
    therapist if it helps, I don't know, but I am
    telling you to let the FBI handle it from here on
    out.

They both stand opposite of one another,
everything happening unsaid.

SAMMI. Okay, Lily.
LILY. Okay?
SAMMI. Okay.

Lights fade out. The two exit the stage.

Scene 2

In the darkness we hear a man, joyfully singing
an Irish song, as the lights rise on the O'Brien
home we see a wild hair grungy man in jeans, a
hoodie, and a flowery pink apron stirring a
bowl of cookie dough at the counter. There is a
baking mess around the sink and counter, flour
astride, and dozens of cookies sprawled on
cookie sheets and drying racks on the table. He
has an air of absolute confidence and there is
also something very sinister about his grin. On

the couch, neatly piled on one side is a blanket and pillows, as if someone has been sleeping there; a man's jacket has been flung over top.

The door opens and Lily enters carrying a bag full of groceries. She takes her keys out, while talking to Sammi (improv a line here, such as: "Mmmm Sammi that smells amazing…"), as she hip checks the door close. Lily finally looks up and sees the man sitting across from her. The bag drops to the floor, without hesitation, she grabs her gun from her right hip and points it at the man. Sammi is dressed in jeans, a t-shirt, and blazer, her work outfit, including her FBI badge, cuffs, and holster with her weapon. The man continues along without hesitation or fear.

LILY. What the HELL are you doing here?
THE MAN. Well, I —
LILY. –- Shut the fuck up! *(pause)* You're lucky I don't
    shoot you square in the eyes where you stand.
THE MAN. If you would just rel —
LILY. -- Don't! Don't you dare tell me to relax. Don't
    you fucking dare.
THE MAN. Such language for a lady, and one that
    works for the law. Tsk - tsk.
LILY. My language is about to be the least of your
    troubles…Cain.

While keeping her weapon pointed at Cain, she picks up her phone to call her partner.

LILY. Reeves, it's O'Brien, look —

CAIN. I guess you don't care what happens to your
      beautiful wife.

      *Lily slowly lowers the phone, her hand slightly
      shaking, she grips tighter at the gun.*

LILY. What did you say?
CAIN. Your dear sweet Sammi, you know the one, too
      smart for her own good, doesn't know when to
      listen…
LILY. What did you do to her?
CAIN. Nothing…yet.

      *Lily stares at Cain, then hears Reeves and
      raises the phone back to her ear.*

LILY. Sorry, no it's the TV, I just got home and Sam
      must have left it on. *(beat)* Right, I was calling
      because I wanted you to check the Peterson
      case file for me, but I just found it. Yup.
      Thanks, 'night partner.

      Lily hangs up. Pause.

LILY. Is this another one of your games?
CAIN. Check if you don't believe me.

      *Lily never lowering her weapon, dials a
      number and puts the phone to her ear.*

LILY. *Whispering.* Come on, come on...

      *There is no answer. Getting worried, she hangs
      up and dials another number.*

LILY. Hey Lyla, is Sammi in? It's Lily…Oh, she didn't
        come in today… No, yeah I just wanted to tell
        her I am stuck at the office, she must have
        forgotten to call me…That's okay. Thank you
        Lyla, have a good night.

Hanging up, she stares hard at Cain.

LILY. Coincidence, that's all this is.

> *Cain throws a wallet onto the table. The wallet
> lands open id facing up. Lily recognizes it
> instantly. She stumbles back slightly, as she
> lowers her arm, but quickly brings it back up;
> trying desperately not to shoot.*

LILY. Sam…
CAIN. Ready to have a little chit chat?

Cain motions Lily to sit. She doesn't budge.

CAIN. You know these are the best brown buttered
        sugar candied pecan cookies I've ever made.
LILY. *(steady calm)* Choke on it!
CAIN. I get the sense you're angry with me O'Brien.
LILY. Where is Sam?
CAIN. Like I said, she is safe for now. I just wanted to
        have a conversation with my favorite special
        agent. I mean we haven't seen each other since
        the trial. I thought it was time to catch up. By
        the way, did I thank you yet, for making my
        release possible?
LILY. What are you talking about? I had nothing to do
        with that.

CAIN. My mistake…

LILY. Let me make myself very clear, you twisted son of a bitch. I would have done nothing to help you get off.

CAIN. *(Toying with her)* My, my special agent; you do know how I like to get off.

LILY. You know, my finger is way too twitchy for your jokes right about now.

CAIN. Ah, no fun. What happened to your sense of humor O'Brien? I'm just trying to lighten the air in this room…it's so tense.

LILY. Don't.

Lily stares at Cain. He stares back like he is reading her, and then smiles.

CAIN. Man, you really have changed O'Brien…pity. I hate to think you lost your edge, special agent.

LILY. You'll see my edge Cain, when I watch you take your trip down death row after I find new evidence to put you away. And this time, there will be no mistrial, I will watch you burn for Pacey - the right way.

CAIN. Maybe…but not if your dear sweet wifey beats you to the punch.

Lily gives Cain a questionable look, terrified by what he may know.

CAIN. Oh, looks like someone is still in the dark… What a shame to not know what your own wife's up to special agent, someone losing their touch. *(beat)* And here I thought you were on my level O'Brien. That's okay, I'll forgive you.

After all you've been through so much this past year, no one can really blame you for failing at your job just like you failed as a mother.

LILY. Shut Up!

Lily steps one step closer.

LILY. *(unnervingly low voice and calm)* You don't speak about her, you don't mention her again.. Now, if you want to walk out this door without a tote tag, tell me where Sam is, no more stalling, no more games.

CAIN. *(sincerely)* I'm sorry, that was too much. I truly admire you Lily and have felt so connected to you with this little pastime of ours and now you just want it to end, just like that, as if it has meant nothing to you; that's hurtful Lily.

LILY. We have no connection Cain, other than the demented fantasies in your head. Sam!

CAIN. Sam…Sam…Sam. I am talking about us and all you can focus on is Sam.

Cain stares at her menacingly, then goes back to cooking.

CAIN. It's nearly time for you to learn your final lesson and you just can't seem to focus, maybe I can help with that.

LILY. Careful Cain -

CAIN. Impatience. Just another one of life's enablers, tempting people because they are too impatient to wait for things to come to them. But do be patient, your awakening will come all too soon Lily; you've earned it.

LILY. Awakened huh? You're going to set me free…
     from what exactly? What are you trying to
     prove with all this bullshit?
CAIN. Oh Lily, it breaks my heart that after all this
     time…

*A kitchen timer buzzes, interrupting Cain. He
smiles like a little boy, puts a finger up for her
to wait, and pulls out a fresh baked batch of
cookies and places them on the table. Takes a
bite and relishes in it. Then offers her one, she
doesn't flinch. He gets angry for a moment and
grinds the hot cookie in his fist, then turns back
to the smile and lightheartedness from before.*

CAIN. After all this time, you still don't understand
     that all I want is to show you that deep down
     we are the same and capable of bringing true
     justice to the world; we just have different
     means to reach the same end.

*Cain stops baking, and faces her directly,
during this speech he is slowly walking towards
her.*

CAIN. You get to be set free just like me, to do what
     needs to be done to make the world a better
     place, and earn a special place in the afterlife.
     Besides how better to show the world that
     given the right circumstances, even the most
     noble will sacrifice their shield.

*As he walks towards her, Lily is threatening him
to "Stop, stop walking, CAIN!"*

LILY. *(Commanding)* Stop!

Cain finally stops.

LILY. *(scoffing)* That's your big mission, to prove I will take justice in my own hands if necessary? That I would cross the badge if pushed to the edge to serve my own misguided righteousness like you?…I will never. And get something straight, you don't bring justice to the world, you set fire to it.

As she continues to talk, he turns his back and begins to walk away. She notices a soft stuffed grey bunny, and instantly recognizes the little doll; it is Pacey's. As she says the last part of the line, she walks forward gun on him but distracted as she goes to grab the bunny.

LILY. You take from it, but you don't give anything back; that is until your six feet under.

Lily ascertains the bunny but at the cost of herself. Cain is able to take advantage of the opportunity and take her weapon, by twisting her arm behind her back and slipping it out of her grip. He plunges the gun into her back, and holds tightly to her arm.

CAIN. *(Breaking from his calm demeanor full on)* No! I show the world the ugly it tries to push aside and act like it doesn't exist. I deliver children from it to God's warm embrace after giving them purpose, and then cleansing their souls for a pure eternity.

As he continues on, Lily maneuvers to take back her weapon and almost succeeds so he grips tighter and raises the weapon to the back of her head and forces her partly over, making her hold herself up with her other arm straight against the table. He then leads her over to a chair and she pulls away from him, the gun still raised at her now. They have swapped places around the table; he is now by the front door side and she on the kitchen side.

CAIN. I do the real good here, and you will see just how enlightening I can be. For I am close to being done with my mission, it is time for you to rise to the occasion and take my place.

There is a beat as Cain regains his poise. Motions her to sit, she just stares and so he motions again with the gun. She begrudgingly sits, still holding the doll.

CAIN. You set me free Lily…twice…and I am so grateful; I only want to return the favor. I mean what kind of visionaries would we be if we didn't fulfill our purpose.

LILY. You really enjoy hearing yourself talk, don't you?

Unaffected, he stares at her with his knowing grin Lily is sitting away from him and the table, facing forward toward the audience.

CAIN. You - Lily, have far more in common with me than you give yourself credit. You're not as squeaky clean as you like the world to think, are you very…special…agent? *(beat)* I've known you a long time Lily - watched you blossom into a formidable foe…and ally.

LILY. I'd die before being your ally.

CAIN. What about my partner?

Lily stares at Cain, with a silent deadly stare.

LILY. Wow, you have more screws loose than I thought. You may have turned others, but I won't be one of them.

CAIN. But you have already done so much to enlighten those that stand in your way of right and wrong, accurate Agent O'Brien?

Cain grabs a file he had tucked under his coat on the couch, and places it next to her.

CAIN. You understand what most the world is blind to.

LILY. What is this?

CAIN. It's you O'Brien, well, highlights from various cases that may have centered on not so clean endings. You're willing to take short cuts to get the conviction or if you can't, somehow they just happen to fall into precarious situations, no? For- instance look at Dmitri Petrov, you remember him right? He was released and getting away with murder. Money goes a long way in the hands of the corrupt, wouldn't you say; but, miraculously he turned up dead, single shot to the head and conveniently his mistress goes down for the murder, though in all her interviews she swears it wasn't her.

LILY. Murders often swear it wasn't them. Ring a bell

CAIN. Oh, but that's not the only mystery resolve in the bunch. What about Sydney Strassfield who was caught in a fire in her home. You know, the suspected arms dealer responsible for a massacre of *innocent* children in the Sudan, whom just so happens to have all the evidence against her burn up in the evidence locker, and was also about to walk away free as a bird, until her unfortunate accident. *(beat)* Not to mention your partner back when you were a Detective. Shame he had to pay such a steep price which resulted in an opportunistic move to the FBI for you.

This triggers Lily.

CAIN. Convenient, wouldn't you say special Agent? I mean one has to wonder if maybe there's more to the story, or if this is all just a strange coincidence.

LILY. Hmm, using people in the government to pass along information to you. Well, it definitely wouldn't be the first time you weaseled your way in. (looking at Cain, she pushes the file away) Anyway, this file of bullshit you are so desperately clinging to, is merely as you said, "a strange coincidence."

CAIN. I see you.

Cain lays the weapon down on the table, equally between them. Lily takes notices, she

*places the doll by the leg of the chair. Then
slowly stands with her hands on the edge of the
table, creating a full stand-off with her and
Cain.*

LILY. You see what you want to see.
CAIN. You have a funny respect for the law as it is
　　　written by those lesser beings, whereas your
　　　law, you protect beyond all else; as do I.
　　　Sometimes we have to take lives in order to
　　　teach a grander lesson. It's the right and
　　　humane thing to do. I mean hell I already tried
　　　to show you the mirror of your justice when I
　　　released Pacey into the hands of God.

Lily grabs the weapon and points it at Cain.

LILY. Fuck you! You're not really so stupid to believe
　　　that I don't know you well enough to know that
　　　your dirty game always serves you above
　　　anyone else.
CAIN. Aw, you underestimate my mission in this life,
　　　how disheartening. No one measures up to you
　　　Lily, they don't understand me the way you do.
　　　Years of you following my trail, our obsessions
　　　with each other, unparalleled. You know I left
　　　little breadcrumbs and you were the only one
　　　that was cleaver enough to pick up on the
　　　subtleties I left behind.
LILY. Fuck your subtleties. All your conning grandeurs
　　　for this big awakening for me to serve in your
　　　place while you take on the martyrdom role, is
　　　absolute drivel. I will never be you, and you're
　　　not the type to fall on his sword.

CAIN. As you know, people change, like your sweet Sammi for example.

Lily gives Cain a death stare. Cain laughs slightly.

CAIN. *(putting on his jacket)* I think that's my cue to go. Just make sure your little woman stays behind her desk and numbers, unless of course you would like *me* to teach her?

Lily takes a step towards him. Cain grabs a cookie from the baking sheet on the table, and walks towards the door to leave. She keeps her weapon steady.

CAIN. I have to say, these are just superb. If you like, I can leave you the recipe. Though you've never been great at the whole Betty Crocker, June cleaver wifey thing huh. *(Opening the door)* Ya know, it's too bad you couldn't be more of a Suzi homemaker instead of a complicated special agent. But then maybe Pacey and I wouldn't have had our fun.

LILY. *(enraged)* Bastard! You don't get to speak her name. Now, get the fuck out of here before I blow your brains all over the fucking wall.

CAIN. *(Half inside the door)* Temper, temper Lily. It's not time yet -- *patience*, remember? You wouldn't want Sammi's brains splattered all over the wall too would you? Which is what will happen if I don't leave here…unscathed and uncuffed.

LILY. Get out…

Cain smiles knowing he has gotten to her, checkmate, he opens the door to leave, turns back to face Lily. He starts to hand her the file.

CAIN. That file isn't all about you though love, I also included a few extras about your beautiful wifey. It's quite the page turner.

Lily steps towards him. He raises his hand.

CAIN. Unscathed and uncuffed. Let's just say, eyes are always watching.

Cain gives her a wink and leaves. Lily rushes the door and opens it, contemplating going after him but stops. She slams the door and locks it, She walks over to the table staring at the scattered file and fear spreads across her face…the phone rings.

LILY. Sammi!?! *(panic)* Are you okay, where are you?…*(confusion settles over her)* At the office? But I…your wallet…*(she stares intensely at the wallet on the table)* you think you left it…yeah it's on the table. Right, okay, see you soon. Love you…

Lily lowers the phone, standing jolted by everything that has transpired as well as the weighted decision and lies before her. She slowly raises the gun in her hand. Her gaze drifting between the files he left and the gun. Lights fade to black.

Scene 3

The lights rise onto the O'Brien's empty house, which looks disheveled, as if someone was searching for something. By the door there are two suitcases and an overnight bag. On the kitchen table sits an open bag, files, and a sprawled-out case with varying torture tools picked through laying on top. On the counter by the sink, is a bag of chips and a soda next to a paper bag and the beginning of the making of a sandwich; as well as a plate of delicious looking brownies stacked up tall wrapped in plastic. The door to the back rooms is open, like someone is home.

Sammi walks in through the front door, and almost trips over the luggage. Dropping her own bag, she struggles for a moment picking up the bags. Then turns to see the table and stops dead in her tracks. She relooks at the luggage and back to the table, she walks over and picks up the file Cain had previously given to Lily. Lily walks out of the back door holding a toiletry bag, and pauses when she sees Sammi holding the file. Sammi turns to her and they stare at each other, silence. The hurt in both of them too much to surpass with simple words, both frozen, holding pause beyond batted breath of an ending to come.

SAMMI. I am so sorry Lily.
LILY. *(eerily calm)* I know.

SAMMI. I understand this is bad, awful. I did try to let
          it go; I did.
LILY. I know Sam. But you've been lying to me.

Pause

SAMMI. Lily please, I never meant to--
LILY. – Don't…please.

> *Lily goes over to the counter and starts
> spreading peanut butter and jelly on the
> sandwich with loving care.*

LILY. You just couldn't stop yourself, so…I've made
          up my mind.
SAMMI. You're leaving? I can't survive without you.
LILY. If that were true you wouldn't have all of this.
          And those bags are not for me Sam, they're for
          you.
SAMMI. You're kicking me out?!?
LILY. Not quite.

> *Lily has been putting together the sandwich,
> chips, the drink, and an apple in the sack
> during this time, like a mother for her child.
> Sammi stops her.*

SAMMI. What the hell does that mean Lily?

> *Lily pauses in thought, she looks at Sammi and
> has second thoughts, but then sees the file on
> the table and looks back, this time with fire in
> her eyes.*

LILY. I promise what I am doing is for your own good.
      Because I love you.
SAMMI. You're scaring me a little.

Long Pause

LILY. I'm having you committed.

      *Sammi is taken back. Lily moves past her to put
      the lunch in one of the bags by the door.
      Suddenly Sammi laughs uncomfortably.*

SAMMI. Excuse me? How do you think you could
       even make that stick? You can't… I'm clearly
       not insane.
LILY. *(pointing to the table)* No? Well, I think I could
      make quite the case to the contrary.
SAMMI. You can't be serious; this has to be a joke.
LILY. Not a very funny one.

      Lily moves back to counter to clean up.

SAMMI. No it's not. And besides, after a 72-hour hold
       I'd be out and you couldn't stop me from doing
       it then, but you sure as shit would break my
       damn trust.
LILY. Statements like that aren't helping your case.
      Anyways, I don't need a 72-hour hold. I'm the
      FBI, remember? And don't get me started about
      breaking trust, I mean really?
SAMMI. I haven't committed a crime.
LILY. Semantics.
SAMMI. So you would rather have your wife
       committed, than help me take revenge on the

thing that brutally killed our daughter? I just want to make sure I have that correct.

LILY. No Sammi, I would rather save you from both yourself and Cain. I am at a loss for how else to stop you.

Sammi is hit hard by this statement. Silence.

LILY. *(finally revealing)* Cain came to see me.

Sammi hit again.

SAMMI. Wait what!?! *(Beat)* Cain was here. He was in our home, our daughter's last place of peace, and you didn't kill him where he stood.?

LILY. Damn it Sam, is that all you can think of? No! I didn't kill the man in cold blood in our dining room, because I would like to keep my badge.

SAMMI. What the hell, Lily? That was your moment, you could have taken down that man for trespassing. What is wrong with you, do you even have a heart?

Sammi's words like a bullet straight through Lily.

LILY. Shame on you. *(Beat)* Aside from the fact that I had no probable cause to shoot him other than trespassing…he said he had YOU somewhere, and I couldn't get ahold of you…Damn you Sam.

SAMMI. Oh—

LILY. – Yeah oh. I called your work and they said you hadn't come in that day. I thought he was going

to kill you, and you're right, I didn't have the
heart to challenge that notion; especially when
he had your wallet.

SAMMI. My wallet? I told you I had forgotten to take
it with me.

LILY. Clearly.

Pause

LILY. By the way, I am totally fine after that
experience, thanks for asking.

Lily walks away. Her back stays to Sammi.

SAMMI. I'm sorry my love, truly. I just get a little
crazy when it comes to Cain.

LILY. Ya think? You're so consumed by anger, that you
can no longer differentiate between right and
wrong. And you've lost sight of me in the
process.

*Sammi wraps her arms around Lily. Lily melts
into her embrace.*

SAMMI. That's not true Lily. I love you so much. I
didn't mean for you to find out this way. I was
going to tell you before…but to have me
committed to stop me, that is nuts. I just need a
little more time to figure things out.

*Lily broken by this statement, pushes Sammi
away.*

LILY. You can't seem to acknowledge that Cain will win in all this despite what is right in front of you. You are playing into his hands; he knows what you're doing, what you're planning!

SAMMI. How can he?

LILY. He has his ways. Cain was here to warn me.

SAMMI. Warn you about what? Me?

LILY. Yes, Sammi!

Sammi gives her a strange look.

LILY. He is insane to a level you can't begin to understand. Cain has a reason for everything in his twisted mind. He basically held a fucked-up business meeting in his mind by holding me hostage in our home with threats of your life, simply to inform me that he doesn't want you to kill him. He was very clear that if I am unable to stop you, he will take it upon himself to do so.

SAMMI. I am not afraid of him!

LILY. *(besides herself)* Then you haven't been paying attention. Crazy always wins because they are willing to go places you can't begin to fathom. To break every line, as they don't exist to them in the first place. Only the lines of right and wrong that he designs hold any weight for him.

SAMMI. Exactly. You have to match crazy with crazy.

LILY. But you're not crazy! I am through with this, do you hear me? I don't know how to keep you safe anymore. Especially when I am not here to protect you, or keep you from going off on some cock- eyed plan that will get yourself killed. So decide right here, right now…it's me and you, or it's this--

Lily points to the luggage.

LILY. – but either way, this is the moment when you decide the type of woman you want to be.

A moment of silence lingers, then Sammi walks over to Lily. They stand silently together. Sammi takes her into her arms, gives her a gentle kiss, and places her forehead together with Lily; their eyes closed. They say so much without a word spoken, a ritual they have done forever to say I am sorry. Lily at peace at last. After a few minutes of silence, Sam whispers.

SAMMI. I'm sorry Lily, Pacey needs me more.

Lily melts with grief for all is lost and now what she must do, there is no road back. Sammi pulls away and begins to grab her purse she had thrown earlier on the couch, her back to Lily. Lily stands heart wrenched and places her hand in her pocket.

LILY. *(whispering)* I'm sorry too Sam…

Lily discreetly pulls out a needle from her pocket and plunges it into Sammi's neck, her eyes burst open. Sammi grabs her neck and then stumbles back with surprise and fear as she looks at Lily. She tries to speak but is incapable. Sammi falls back and slides down the wall, her eyes close, and her hands drop to her side. Lily bends down and kisses her on the cheek.

LILY. I will take care of Cain, and then I will tell Pacey that her mommy is still one of the good ones.

Lily brushes Sammi's hair out of her eyes and sweetly kisses her on the forehead.

LILY. I love you.

Blackout.

End of Play.